ESB

D0217191

ENVIRONMENTAL JUSTICE AND RESILIENCY IN AN AGE OF UNCERTAINTY

This book examines the issue of environmental justice across 11 short chapters, with the aim of creating a resilient society.

Starting with a history of the environmental justice movement, the book then moves on to focus on various current environmental issues, analyzing how these issues impact low-income and minority communities. Topics covered include smart cities and environmental justice, climate change and health equity, the Flint Water Crisis, coastal resilience, emergency management, energy justice, procurement and contract management, public works projects, and the impact of COVID-19. Each chapter provides a unique perspective on the issues covered, offering practical strategies to create a more resilient society that can be applied by practitioners in the field.

Environmental Justice and Resiliency in an Age of Uncertainty will be of interest to upper level undergraduate and graduate students studying race relations, environmental politics and policy, sustainability, and social justice. It will also appeal to practitioners working at all levels of government, and anyone with an interest in environmental issues, racial justice, and the construction of resilient communities.

Celeste Murphy-Greene, PhD, MPA, is a faculty member and program coordinator for the graduate certificates in Public Administration, and Leadership at the University of Virginia. Over a 25-year career, Murphy-Greene has worked at the US Environmental Protection Agency and as a congressional aide, before moving into academia. Her research focuses on environmental policy, local government financial management, and quality of life issues. Her work has appeared in *Public Administration Review, International Journal of Public Administration, Public Administration Quarterly, Journal of Health and Human Services Administration, Review of Policy Research, Journal of Business and Public Affairs,* and *Journal of Emergency Management.*

"Wildfires, floods, droughts, and pandemics beget pollution, drowning, starvation, and deaths. And they affect marginalized communities worst. This book explains how it happens and what to do about it. It explains vulnerabilities caused by climate change and what real environmental justice would look like. Read it to get up-to-date information on how communities can work toward environmental justice and build resilience into mitigation efforts. Traditional topics are covered as well as new dimensions, filling a niche for environmental policy and social equity courses."

Mary E. Guy, *University of Colorado Denver*

"The world faces numerous crises implicating environmental justice, such as global climate change, the COVID-19 pandemic, resource depredation, structural inequities, and more. The need for accountability for environmental justice has never been more acute, especially to understand the causes and effects of these injustices and to diversely, equitably, and inclusively forge new ways forward. Celeste Murphy-Greene has brought together an authoritative group of authors—both practitioners and academics—to examine critical environmental justice topics and to share tools that can help foster resiliency and a better future for all. Anyone interested in equity and justice should read and apply the lessons from this text."

Sean McCandless, *University of Illinois Springfield*

"As the leader of an organization that prioritizes energy transition research and other public impact initiatives aimed at bringing about change in historically disadvantaged communities, this book is informative yet practical in offering possible solutions for those interested in addressing environmental justice. The authors paint an illuminating picture of how our social, economic, and community well-being is inextricably linked to our ability to acknowledge the historical injustices that have been institutionalized across the country, while also giving us hope for how we can be more environmentally equitable even as we continue to navigate the uncertainties of the 'new normal'."

Larry D. Terry, *University of Virginia*

"Climate action and sustainability plans must prioritize equity and inclusion. To manage the climate crisis equitably it is imperative that communities work to resolve environmental justice challenges. Cities are charged with this critical task and leadership is needed to ensure this is accomplished. This book offers important insights for community leaders into the impacts of the climate crisis on disadvantaged populations and a path forward towards building resiliency. It is well researched and provides a comprehensive look at the challenges and what must be done to resolve them."

Lori Welch, *City of Lansing, Sustainability Manager*

"The racism entrenched in the systems and structures of our communities is exposed by the sound research, data, and case studies in Dr. Greene's new book. The recent focus has been on racial injustice and police. Dr. Greene's collection, however, illustrates that equity issues are far more pervasive: healthcare, emergency management, public works, zoning, and others. Most importantly, the authors present insights and solutions. Local leaders who care about equity will find helpful guidance in this research."

Ron Carlee, *Old Dominion University*

"This Emergency Management text addresses environmental and climate justice issues, COVID-19, health equity, community resilience, and more in these challenging times with natural and biological disasters. The text further prepares students for solutions such as building resilient and smart communities, focusing on clean energy, and disaster preparedness. I highly recommend this textbook because it walks the reader through a series of important environmental issues, focusing on equity in a way that prepares them for interacting with diverse communities."

Charlyn A. Hilliman, *Capella University*

"Environmental Justice and Resiliency in an Age of Uncertainty is a must read for sustainability and resiliency practitioners who want to bring environmental justice focus to their work. In this seminal work, the authors take readers through the historical events and current cultural factors surrounding the most pressing environmental justice issues we face, detail how the accelerating climate crisis and Covid-19 pandemic have exacerbated these challenges, and outline the tools and resources we can use to work toward a more resilient and equitable future."

Annette Osso, *LEED AP, Managing Director, Resilient Virginia*

ENVIRONMENTAL JUSTICE AND RESILIENCY IN AN AGE OF UNCERTAINTY

Edited by Celeste Murphy-Greene

NEW YORK AND LONDON

Cover image: © Getty Images

First published 2022
by Routledge
605 Third Avenue, New York, NY 10158

and by Routledge
4 Park Square, Milton Park, Abingdon, Oxon, OX14 4RN

Routledge is an imprint of the Taylor & Francis Group, an informa business

© 2022 selection and editorial matter, Celeste Murphy-Greene; individual chapters, the contributors

The right of Celeste Murphy-Greene to be identified as the author of the editorial material, and of the authors for their individual chapters, has been asserted in accordance with sections 77 and 78 of the Copyright, Designs and Patents Act 1988.

All rights reserved. No part of this book may be reprinted or reproduced or utilised in any form or by any electronic, mechanical, or other means, now known or hereafter invented, including photocopying and recording, or in any information storage or retrieval system, without permission in writing from the publishers.

Trademark notice: Product or corporate names may be trademarks or registered trademarks, and are used only for identification and explanation without intent to infringe.

Library of Congress Cataloging-in-Publication Data
A catalog record for this title has been requested

ISBN: 978-1-032-02450-9 (hbk)
ISBN: 978-1-032-02449-3 (pbk)
ISBN: 978-1-003-18607-6 (ebk)

DOI: 10.4324/9781003186076

Typeset in Bembo
by Newgen Publishing UK

I dedicate this book to my family including my parents, Martha and Fred Murphy, whose love and support has been a constant source of strength throughout my life and my husband, Kevin, and sons, William and Nolan, who I feel grateful to have in my life.

CONTENTS

FIGURES

CONTRIBUTORS

Michael A. Brown, PhD, is the president of the nonprofit policy institute One World One Way, Inc. that provides consultation on business continuity plans for private industry, disaster and emergency management, and the building of resilient and sustainable communities using hazard mitigation and environmental justice. Brown provides guidance on unmanned aircraft systems and protection of critical infrastructure to strengthen communities. Brown served in the US Air Force as a combat crew member, nuclear weapons officer, and intelligence operations specialist. Brown has a Master Certification in Critical Infrastructure Protection (CIP) and is a subject matter expert in emergency management processes. He served as Core Faculty Emergency Management Professor at Capella University School of Public Service Schools of Leadership. Brown is currently slated to be Chair of Emergency Management Education, Project Good Hope, US Virgin Islands.

Seth Mullendore, MS, is President for Clean Energy Group, a national nonprofit organization accelerating an equitable and inclusive transition to a resilient, sustainable clean energy future. Through his work with Clean Energy Group, Seth oversees projects ranging from customer-sited solar and battery storage to the replacement of power plants with clean technologies. Seth works with community-based organizations, environmental justice groups, policy makers, project developers, industry leaders, and advocates to advance innovative clean energy policy and facilitate the development of community-serving projects, with a focus on achieving greater access to solar and battery storage technologies for low-income communities and communities of color. Seth holds a MS in Civil and Environmental Engineering from Stanford University, and a BS in Geosciences from the University of Southern Maine.

Celeste Murphy-Greene, PhD, MPA, is the founder of the Graduate Certificate in Public Administration at the University of Virginia's School of Continuing and Professional Studies, where she currently serves as Faculty and Program Coordinator. She also serves as a Program Coordinator for UVA's Graduate Certificate in Leadership and is an Adjunct Faculty Member at Adler University's Master of Public Administration Program, where she teaches sustainability. Before her over 25-year career in academia, Murphy-Greene worked at the US Environmental Protection Agency and served as a Legislative Aide on Capitol Hill. Her research focuses on environmental justice, local government financial management, and quality of life issues. Murphy-Greene has written many peer-reviewed journal articles and book chapters. Her work has appeared in *Public Administration Review, International Journal of Public Administration, Public Administration Quarterly, Journal of Health and Human Services Administration, Review of Policy Research, Journal of Business and Public Affairs, and Journal of Emergency Management.*

Angela Orebaugh, PhD, is passionate about technology and sustainability and the synergies between them to address wicked problems. She is faculty at the University of Virginia where she teaches courses in cybersecurity, smart cities, and sustainability. She completed her PhD in Information Technology at George Mason University and Master of Liberal Arts in Sustainability at Harvard University. Orebaugh is a certified WELL AP and completed a certificate in Green Building and Community Sustainability at Harvard University and a certificate in Sustainable Business at UVA's McIntire School of Business. Her interests include cybersecurity, smart cities, the Internet of Things, and green building. Orebaugh is an internationally recognized author of several bestselling technology books, author of over 30 published articles, and co-author of 7 National Institute of Standards and Technology (NIST) publications. As a Board Member for Resilient Virginia and SmartCville, Orebaugh focuses on promoting the use of technology to make cities a better place to live.

James W. Patteson, MPA, lives in Fairfax, Virginia, where he spent 35 years working for the county's Public Works Department—ten years as its director. He was recognized by the American Public Works Association (APWA) as a Top 10 Leader in 2018 and received an Engineering Excellence Award from George Mason University Civil Engineering Institute in 2019. James serves on APWA's Center for Sustainability where he advocates for improving the nation's infrastructure. While working for Fairfax County, James created a strong focus on building sustainable solutions that address the social, economic, and environmental needs of the community. James is a registered professional engineer with a BS in Civil and Environmental Engineering from Virginia Tech and a Masters in Public Administration from George Mason University.

Janet A. Phoenix, MD, MPH, is an assistant research professor in the Departments of Health Policy and Management in the Milken Institute School of Public Health at George Washington University in Washington, DC. Phoenix conducts research in children's environmental health, with an emphasis on community-based participatory methods such as health impact analysis. She is a physician by training who has managed research, risk communication, and health prevention and promotion programs for many organizations. She received her BA in Anthropology from the University of Colorado in Denver and her MD from Howard University. Phoenix also completed a Master's degree in Public Health from the Bloomberg School of Public Health in Baltimore. She currently serves on the Board of the Healthy Schools Network and Clean Air Partners. She was appointed by the Governor of Virginia to serve on the Advisory Council on Environmental Justice for the State of Virginia. She was elected to Chair that body in 2018.

Jim Redick, MPA, is the Director of Emergency Preparedness and Response for the City of Norfolk, VA. He is a Certified Emergency Manager with the International Association of Emergency Managers (IAEM) and in 2017 was recognized by the Virginia Emergency Management Association with the Stanley Everett Crigger Humanitarian Achievement Award. He earned his Bachelor of Science in Organizational Leadership and Management from Regent University and a Master's degree in Public Administration from Old Dominion University. Redick is also a graduate of FEMA's Advanced and Executive Academies and the Naval Postgraduate School's Center of Homeland Defense and Security Executive Leadership Program.

Cara Sanner, BA, a native Michigander born in Detroit and raised in southeast Michigan, celebrates 25 years of service with positions in both the public and nonprofit sectors. Cara spent the first 15 years of her professional career in mid-Michigan, working to advance sustainability practices and resource conservation in her roles with the City of Lansing, the Michigan Recycling Coalition, and Clinton County. She later moved to central Virginia, where she works to support best practices and policies in professional regulation with the international non-profit, the Association of Social Work Boards. Cara obtained a Graduate Certificate in Public Administration from the University of Virginia and she holds a Bachelor of Social Sciences from Michigan State University in Interdisciplinary Studies in Community Relations with a Spanish Minor.

Joshua M. Steinfeld, PhD, MS, MPS, is an assistant professor in the Old Dominion University School of Public Service, Director of the Graduate Certificate in Public Procurement and Contract Management at the Strome College of Business, and Director of the Graduate Certificate in Public Sector Leadership at the School of Continuing Education. Steinfeld's research focuses on public procurement, strategic contracting, and source selection. His teaching specializes in leadership and procurement education for executive managers in federal government. He earned his PhD in public administration at Florida Atlantic University, MS in finance at Johns Hopkins University, MPS in organizational leadership at University of Denver, and BSBA in organizational behavior at Boston University. His favorite part of the job is mentoring students toward the achievement of their career goals.

Chris R. Surfus, PhD, is a postdoctoral research associate at the University of New Hampshire's Institute on Disability in the NIDILRR-funded ARRT program. He graduated in June 2021 with a PhD in Public Administration from Western Michigan University's School of Public Affairs and Administration. He has a Master of Public Administration, Master of Business Administration, and Graduate Certificate in Nonprofit Leadership from Grand Valley State University. He has presented at multiple regional and national conferences. Surfus is the current President of the ASPA Michigan Capital Area Chapter, and he is also the President of The Surfus Foundation, which works on LGBTQ+. Much of his research is on LGBTQ+ policy and administration, racial equity, municipal government topics, environmental justice, and COVID-19.

ACKNOWLEDGMENTS

This book has been over three years in the making. The idea came about during a resilience forum I attended at Old Dominion University. Since that time, our world has changed greatly with the ongoing pandemic and the impact it has had on communities throughout the world. I am extremely grateful for all the contributing authors who have shared their knowledge and experience in the following chapters. Their persistence, patience, and hard work turned this book from an idea into a reality.

I also offer special thanks to those who have mentored me throughout my career, when I first started researching and writing about environmental justice back in the early 1990s. Dr. Leslie Leip, who served as the chair of my doctoral dissertation committee, provided strength and wisdom as I was beginning my academic career. My former colleague and department chair, Dr. Roberta Walsh, has been a source of constant support and encouragement both personally and professionally.

Finally, I offer special appreciation to the editors at Routledge who believed in this book from the beginning. Thank you for supporting this important endeavor.

INTRODUCTION

Celeste Murphy-Greene

These are truly uncertain times. At the time of this writing, the COVID-19-induced pandemic has ravaged the US and global community for over a year and a half. Vaccination rates are still not at the levels needed to attain herd immunity as many are hesitant of what they perceive as "unknown" long-term impacts of the vaccine. As communities work to regain a sense of normalcy, what is now normal is redefined as the "new normal." This "new normal" includes wearing masks in schools and many indoor locations. Many wonder: When will the pandemic be over? When will things get back to normal? The ongoing pandemic has highlighted many pre-existing conditions of social, economic, and environmental inequity that have existed in the United States and globally for decades. Minorities and low-income individuals have had to bear the brunt of environmental pollution for decades and are currently suffering disproportionately from the effects of COVID-19.

While reigning in COVID-19 is a priority, it has shifted the focus from the greater crisis at hand, which is climate change. As our climate changes, more extreme weather events become the "new normal." Much like the impacts of COVID-19, climate change also disproportionately impacts the most vulnerable populations in the United States and globally, and those communities least prepared to cope with social and economic disruptions caused by extreme weather events. This book explores pressing issues our society faces today and those pre-existing inequities and offers strategies to help address them to help build stronger and more resilient communities.

Resilient communities are those best able to recover from social, economic, and environmental disruptions. Resiliency is the ability to bounce back to normal after facing a difficulty. Many communities throughout the United States and globally have demonstrated resiliency in the face of adversity for decades. This is not new.

DOI: 10.4324/9781003186076-1

However, what is new is the unprecedented environmental issues our country and world face today. As record wildfires destroy thousands of acres of California's forests and leave many homeless, many more are displaced in Haiti after another hurricane wreaks havoc on an already fragile society. This book addresses today's pressing environmental issues using a justice lens.

The environmental justice movement can be described as the intersection of the environmental and civil rights movements, focusing on the environment and social justice as one. While environmental justice is not a new term, it has gained recognition in recent years. What began as a grassroots environmental movement in the 1980s is now a major national and international issue. I first began researching and writing about environmental justice in graduate school in the early 1990s. My research has focused on examining environmental justice from the occupational perspective of migrant farmworkers to global environmental justice issues.

This book *Environmental Justice and Resiliency in an Age of Uncertainty* provides a framework to address the many pressing environmental issues our nation and global community face today. Chapter 1, An Overview of Environmental Justice, provides an introduction to environmental justice including a reflection on the history of the environmental justice movement and current advancements at the federal, state, and local levels. This chapter explores the factors that make up an environmental justice community and how to address those factors.

Chapter 2, Climate Justice and Vulnerable Populations, examines how climate change disproportionately impacts the most vulnerable populations in the United States and globally including the poor, elderly, and those least able to cope with extreme weather events. The issue of Urban Heat Islands is explored as well as the practice of redlining and how this historic practice further exacerbates "pre-existing" social and public health issues.

The issue of public health is examined in more depth in Chapter 3, COVID-19: Addressing Health Equity in the United States. The pandemic has had the greatest impact and taken the greatest toll on minority populations. Additionally, those communities have lower vaccination rates than the general population. The issue of vaccine hesitancy will be examined as well as cultural and historic reasons for the lack of trust within minority communities for the public health system.

The Flint Water Crisis is the focus of Chapter 4. This man-made public health crisis is a disaster of historic proportions. Thousands of people in the City of Flint, Michigan were poisoned by their own drinking water due to a decision made by local officials to change the water source for the community. As a large minority and low-income community, Flint represents one of the more egregious cases of environmental injustice in the United States. This chapter reviews the timeline of the crisis and offers solutions to avoid future disasters.

Chapter 5, Anti-Resilience Factors of Environmental Justice Communities, focuses on the many factors that work against communities achieving environmental justice. These factors include education, health, housing, and zoning laws that impede a community's ability to achieve its fullest potential.

Smart Cities is the focus of Chapter 6. Today's cities are implementing tools and practices that both encourage sustainability and include an equity lens. Addressing environmental justice concerns with new technology allows innovation to work to the advantage of those most impacted by the brunt of environmental pollution.

Our world is in the midst of an energy revolution and energy justice is a newly emerging field within the clean energy sector. Chapter 7, Advancing Energy Justice Through Local Clean Energy, provides examples of how clean energy is helping the most disadvantaged members of our society using several cutting-edge examples from California. As drought-induced wildfires continue to ravage California, energy has been the focus of the cause of several of the fires. Additionally, power is often shutoff to prevent future fires during extreme weather. Energy justice provides local clean energy solutions to communities in need.

As extreme weather becomes a more common occurrence, the role of emergency management is of growing importance. Chapter 8 explores the role of emergency management in addressing the needs of all community members, especially those most vulnerable, in the face of extreme weather. A strategic emergency management plan, with an equity and justice lens, is a necessity for building resilient communities.

As communities focus on preparing for extreme weather, infrastructure takes center stage. Chapter 9, Public Works—A Partner to Build More Equitable Communities, offers several case studies demonstrating the important role public works projects play in building resilient communities by incorporating the needs of all community members. This chapter explores the role of quality public infrastructure and facilities such as roads, bridges, and green spaces such as parks.

Chapter 10, Public Procurement and Contract Management for Environmental Justice and Resiliency, examines how the government and private sector strive toward improving environmental justice using collaborative contracting and procurement practices. This chapter offers examples from the federal and state government and private sector.

In closing, this book covers a wide range of topics, written by a mix of practitioners and researchers, with real-world experience and knowledge providing useful strategies and tools to help communities address both environmental justice and resiliency. The examples and case studies serve as guides for all communities. While nobody can predict the future, having useful tools to help prepare for what the future may bring while addressing current inequities, will help create stronger and more resilient communities for years to come.

1

AN OVERVIEW OF ENVIRONMENTAL JUSTICE

Celeste Murphy-Greene

Introduction

In recent years, the environmental justice movement has gained much momentum. What several years ago was rarely mentioned in the media or by policy makers is now considered a mainstream environmental issue. The social unrest of the summer of 2020 called attention to the inequities faced by minorities in all facets of life, including the environment. This chapter will discuss the difference between equality, equity, and justice, the factors that lead to the creation of an environmental justice community, and provide an overview of the environmental justice movement from its origin to the present day. While they sound similar, there is a definite distinction between equality, equity, and justice. Equality focuses on equal treatment of all. Applying an equality principle to society would assume everyone benefits from equal resources regardless of their individual needs. However, equality fails to meet the unique and varying needs of all individuals. Equity focuses on providing everyone the resources they need, based on the needs of the individuals. Affirmative action is an example of equity in action. Justice removes systematic barriers causing inequity. Justice is based on the principle that individuals do not need accommodations or supports because the barriers or factors causing the inequity have been removed. When applying the justice principle to the environment, the US Environmental Protection Agency (US EPA) defines environmental justice as follows:

> The fair treatment and meaningful involvement of all people regardless of race, color, national origin, or income with respect to the development, implementation, and enforcement of environmental laws, regulations, and policies.

DOI: 10.4324/9781003186076-2

Fair treatment means that no group of people, including racial, ethnic, or socioeconomic group should bear a disproportionate share of the negative environmental consequences resulting from industrial, municipal, and commercial operations or the execution of federal, state, local and tribal programs and policies.

US EPA, 2021a

The three main focus areas of environmental justice are: (1) The distribution of the effect of environmental pollution, (2) the environmental policy-making process, and (3) the administration of environmental protection programs. Thus, environmental justice focuses on the fairness of environmental procedures, taking a participatory approach to the development, implementation, and enforcement of environmental protection programs. This involves recognizing historic causes of inequities, and working with administrative agencies and diverse groups to address these injustices.

Social Vulnerability and Environmental Justice

There are many factors that lead to the creation of an environmental justice community. In order to better understand what an environmental justice community looks like, one must explore the issue of social vulnerability. According to the Agency for Toxic Substances and Disease Registry, social vulnerability refers to "the resilience of communities (the ability to survive and thrive) when confronted by external stresses on human health, stresses such as natural or human-caused disasters, or disease outbreaks. Reducing social vulnerability can decrease both human suffering and economic loss" (Agency for Toxic Substances and Disease Registry, 2021). It is important to understand a community's social vulnerability risk to disasters as well as chronic issues such as environmental pollution. Environmental pollution is a risk factor contributing to health problems in communities throughout the United States and globally (Murphy-Greene, 2007, 2010; Murphy-Greene & Leip, 2002).

The Social Distance Model in Figure 1.1 helps illustrate the factors that contribute to a community's vulnerability, leading to exposure to environmental pollution. Social Distance Indicators include: (1) One's income, (2) education, (3) property ownership, (4) use of the dominant language, (5) laws and their legal rights, and (6) race/ethnicity of the individual. When there is a negative outcome for the Social Distance Indictors, it leads to: (1) Poverty, (2) alienation, (3) lack of skills, (4) economic exploitation, (5) lack of use of the dominant language, (6) lack of information on laws and legal rights, and (7) few choices and alternatives for employment and housing. The combination of negative outcomes of these indicators leads to a vulnerable community at risk of exposure to environmental hazards and a lack of protection from environmental laws. Environmental risk factors come in many forms including pollution released in the air from factories

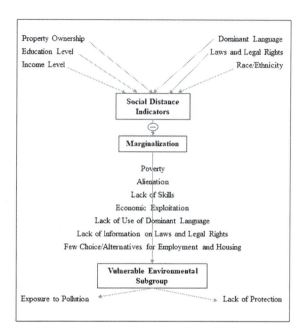

FIGURE 1.1 Social Distance Model

and cars, toxic chemicals disposed of in waterways and on land, and pesticides from agricultural applications. Communities at greater risk of exposure to environmental pollution are referred to as environmental justice communities. In order to address the environmental inequities that exist throughout the United States, the environmental justice movement evolved. This chapter will now discuss the evolution of the environmental justice movement from its inception to today.

Beginning of the Environmental Justice Movement

In 1971, the Council on Environmental Quality issued a report acknowledging the impacts of racial discrimination on the urban poor and their environment (Bryant & Mohai, 1992). This report is the first national recognition of racial disparities when examining the impacts of environmental pollution. However, the event that sparked the environmental justice movement is the 1982 Warren County, North Carolina protest of a hazardous waste landfill. This grassroots protest gained national attention and is considered by many the seminal event in the environmental justice movement.

The environmental justice movement has made tremendous progress since it began in 1982. The Warren County protest set off a chain of events at the national level. In response to the Warren County, NC protest, in 1983, the General Accounting Office (now the Government Accountability Office [GAO]) issued a report citing Blacks were disproportionately impacted by hazardous landfills in the South (US EPA Region 4). This GAO report led to a 1987 study by the United Church of Christ that found race was the most significant variable tested in association with the location of commercial hazardous waste facilities (United Church of Christ, 1987).

Also, in the 1980s, Chicago resident and community activist, Hazel Johnson, an African American woman, worked to alert city, state, and national policy makers of the health problems plaguing her community after her husband's early death from cancer. Ms. Johnson discovered there was a high incidence of cancer in her community, the Altgeld Gardens housing project, which she labeled a toxic doughnut due to the many landfills and polluted air surrounding her neighborhood. She founded the grassroots organization, People for Community Recovery. Her community organizing efforts helped address issues facing her housing complex such as asbestos within the walls of the buildings and cyanide and other toxins in the drinking water. In 1992, Ms. Johnson was awarded the President's Environment and Conservation Challenge Award by President Bill Clinton. Ms. Johnson, who died in 2011, made a significant contribution to the environmental justice movement and is considered the "Mother of Environmental Justice" (Rush, 2019).

Robert Bullard (1990), who is considered the "Grandfather of the Environmental Justice Movement," published the book *Dumping in Dixie*, what is considered the first book on environmental justice. In it, Bullard blames the government at all levels for institutional racism and discriminatory land-use policies and practices. Dr. Bullard has written extensively on environmental justice and has been a major force in the environmental justice movement. Also in 1990, the University of Michigan held a conference titled *Conference on Race and the Incidence of Environmental Hazards*. This conference gathered academics and policy makers to address environmental inequities in minority communities.

The National Law Journal article by Coye and Lavelle (1992) illustrated racial divide in the way the US government cleaned up toxic waste sites and punished polluters. The authors argued White communities saw faster action, better results, and stiffer penalties than minority communities.

US Environmental Protection Agency and Environmental Justice

In response to growing evidence of environmental health inequities throughout the United States, in 1992, the US EPA created the Environmental Equity Workgroup. This workgroup was charged with examining the issue of what was then called environmental equity. In 1992, the US EPA established the Office of Environmental Equity. In 1993, the name was changed to the Office of Environmental Justice. The Director of the Office of Environmental Justice was an African American woman named Dr. Clarice Gaylord. Dr. Gaylord conveyed the challenges of directing this newly established office. Dr. Gaylord stated: "I was

given a big title but very little funding. I had to go to Congress asking for money"
(Gaylord, personal communication). In addition to the challenge of obtaining
funding for the newly created Office of Environmental Justice, Dr. Gaylord was
charged with assembling a staff and working to address environmental justice
within each agency and federal department.

To help guide the EPA in advancing environmental justice, the National
Environmental Justice Advisory Council (NEJAC) was established in 1993.
NEJAC consists of 25 members appointed from stakeholder groups representing
community members, academics, business, tribal governments, non-government
organizations (NGOs), and state and local governments. The goal of NEJAC is to
provide independent advice to the US EPA on environmental justice.

FEDERAL POLICIES SUPPORTING ENVIRONMENTAL JUSTICE

President Clinton Signs Executive Order 12898

A major step in the environmental justice movement was in 1994 when President
Bill Clinton signed *Executive Order 12898: Federal Actions to Address Environmental
Justice in Minority and Low-Income Populations* (US EPA, 2021b). This Executive
Order (EO) was the first federal policy addressing environmental justice. EO
12898 requires all federal agencies and departments to develop and execute a plan
to address environmental justice and led to the establishment of the Interagency
Working Group (IWG), chaired by the EPA administrator. The IWG comprises
the heads of 11 cabinet-level federal departments and agencies such as the Justice
Department, the Office of Management and Budget, the Office of Science and
Technology, the Department of Agriculture, the Department of Transportation, the
Department of Health and Human Services, and the Department of Commerce.
The IWG meets monthly to continue work on collaborative projects addressing
environmental justice.

Following the signing of EO 12898, the challenge for the US EPA and all the
federal agencies and departments was how best to implement this new policy. In
1995, the US EPA issued the *Environmental Justice Strategy: Executive Order 12898*.
This provided a set of goals and objectives for the agencies to help achieve environmental justice. In 1997, the EPA released the *Environmental Justice Implementation
Plan*. This provided a framework for achieving the environmental justice goals
established by the agency. One of the main policies the US EPA is charged
with implementing is the National Environmental Policy Act (NEPA). This law
requires all agencies conducting projects that may impact the environment to
complete an Environmental Impact Statement (EIS). In order for the EPA to fully
integrate environmental justice principles into the work of the agency, environmental justice goals had to be incorporated into the preparation of each EIS and
Environmental Assessment (EA). Therefore, incorporating environmental justice

into the development of each EIS and EA was part of the *Environmental Justice Implementation Plan*.

Challenges Implementing Executive Order 12898

One of the main challenges implementing EO 12898 is maintaining the support from each presidential administration. As administrations change with the election of a new president, the current administration chooses to continue or discontinue the previous administration's policies. EOs can be overturned or weakened by a new president, depending on their policy objectives. While the Clinton Administration strongly supported environmental justice at the US EPA, the Bush Administration, taking office in 2001, did not place environmental justice as a high priority. In 2004, the Office of Inspector General Report criticized the US EPA for not implementing EO 12898, and in 2005, the General Accountability Office also criticized the EPA for the lack of implementation of EO 12898. During the Bush Administration, the Northwest Regional Office of Environmental Justice was closed.

The Obama Administration restored a focus on environmental justice. Lisa Jackson, appointed by President Barack Obama, made environmental justice a top priority of the EPA. As the first African American to lead the agency, in January 2010, the EPA issued a report, *Expanding the Conversation on Environmentalism and Working for Environmental Justice*. In July 2010, the EPA issued *Plan EJ 2014*, a new roadmap for the EPA to achieve environmental justice priorities. This plan commemorated the 20th anniversary of the signing of EO 12898.

Under the Trump Administration, the Office of Environmental Justice experienced a major overhaul. Several longtime staffers resigned their positions in response to the anti-environmental rhetoric espoused by the Trump Administration. The EPA experienced turmoil under the Trump Administration with one of the EPA administrators, Scott Pruitt, resigning halfway through his tenure due to ethics violations (Perls, 2021). Despite these challenges, the EPA was able to continue offering its Small Grants Program providing funding to community organizations at the local level. Additionally, the EPA launched an interactive environmental justice tool called EJScreen. This tool allows individuals to log onto the EJScreen website and find information related to a location's proximity to hazardous waste, a Superfund site, and lead paint. See the EJScreen resource link at the back of this chapter.

The Biden Administration, taking office in January 2021, placed environmental justice as a top priority, appointing Michael Regan, the first African American male to lead the agency. Mr. Regan, the former director of North Carolina's Department of Environmental Quality, made environmental justice a top priority in North Carolina. Due to Mr. Regan's strong track-record on environmental justice, he was selected to run the US EPA. Mr. Regan is quoted as saying:

> We will be driven by our convictions that every person in our great country has the right to clean air, clean water and a healthier life, no matter how much money they have in their pockets, the color of their skin or the community that they live in.
>
> *Barnett, 2020*

Additionally, within the first 100 days in office, President Biden established the White House Environmental Justice Advisory Council (WHEJAC) (White House, 2021). This council includes community members, academics, and state and local officials from around the United States. The WHEJAC held its first meeting virtually on March 30, 2021.

In addition to creating the WHEJAC, on January 27, 2021, President Biden signed EO 14008: Tackling the Climate Crisis at Home and Abroad. This EO addresses national and global environmental justice issues. One key component of EO 14008 is the establishment of the White House Environmental Justice Interagency Council (WHEJIC).

> The Interagency Council shall develop a strategy to address current and historic environmental injustice by consulting with the White House Environmental Justice Advisory Council and with local environmental justice leaders. The Interagency Council shall also develop clear performance metrics to ensure accountability, and publish an annual public performance scorecard on its implementation.
>
> *White House, 2021, Sec. 219*

The WHEJIC is made up of the heads of federal agencies and departments including the following members: The Attorney General, the Secretary of the Interior, the Secretary of Agriculture, the Secretary of Commerce, the Secretary of Labor, the Secretary of Health and Human Services, the Secretary of Housing and Urban Development, the Secretary of Transportation, the Secretary of Energy, the Chair of the Council of Economic Advisers, the Administrator of the EPA, the Director of the Office of Management and Budget, the Executive Director of the Federal Permitting Improvement Steering Council, the Director of the Office of Science and Technology Policy, the National Climate Advisor, the Assistant to the President for Domestic Policy, and the Assistant to the President for Economic Policy (White House, 2021). The focus of E.O. 14008 on climate change will be discussed in greater detail in Chapter 2.

Federal Civil Rights Laws and Constitutional Rights

In addition to EOs 12898 and 14008, both Title VI of the Civil Rights Act of 1964 and the Fourteenth Amendment to the US Constitution provide legal and

Constitutional tools to help guide the implementation and enforcement of environmental policies in environmental justice communities.

Title VI of the Civil Rights Act of 1964 states:

> Title VI, 42 U.S.C. § 2000d et seq., was enacted as part of the landmark Civil Rights Act of 1964. It prohibits discrimination on the basis of race, color, and national origin in programs and activities receiving federal financial assistance. As President John F. Kennedy said in 1963:
>
> Simple justice requires that public funds, to which all taxpayers of all races [colors, and national origins] contribute, not be spent in any fashion which encourages, entrenches, subsidizes or results in racial [color or national origin] discrimination.
>
> *US Department of Justice, 2021*

Up until 2001, to prove discrimination in environmental cases, one needed to demonstrate a disparate impact of environmental pollution on certain groups. The US Supreme Court weakened Title VI in the 2001 Alexander *v* Sandoval decision, which gutted Title VI of the Civil Rights Act of 1964. This decision calls for the intent rather than disparate impact to prove discrimination. This made environmental justice cases much more challenging to prove in court.

A second policy tool used in environmental justice cases is the Fourteenth Amendment of the US Constitution. The Fourteenth Amendment states:

> No State shall make or enforce any law which shall abridge the privileges or immunities of citizens of the United States; nor shall any State deprive any person of life, liberty, or property without due process of law; nor deny any person within its jurisdiction the equal protection of the laws.
>
> *Farber et al., 1993, Appendix 1, 13*

According to the Fourteenth Amendment of the US Constitution, all citizens of the United States are provided equal protection under the law. The assumption is that the same protections outlined in the US Constitution apply to environmental protection and environmental justice communities.

State Environmental Justice Legislation and Policy

Aside from federal policies, several states have made progress in advancing environmental justice through public policies such as legislation and EOs. Some policies are more far reaching than others. States with an environmental justice policy include: California, Connecticut, New York, Oregon, Rhode Island, Arkansas, Kentucky, Minnesota, North Carolina, and New Mexico. Several of these states such as California have passed specific legislation (AB 617 and SB 673) requiring environmental laws, such as those regulating air quality, to take into consideration the impact of pollution on minority and vulnerable populations. States, such as North Carolina, California, and Virginia, have also formed advisory boards comprising stakeholders including representation from community groups, universities, and non-profit organizations. Other ways states are integrating environmental justice into their policies and practices is through interactive Geographic Information Systems (GIS) mapping sites and environmental grant programs. The State of North Carolina has an excellent community online mapping tool (State of North Carolina, 2021). More progress is being made each year addressing environmental justice at the state level. This will be discussed further in Chapter 2, which focuses on climate justice.

Conclusion

The environmental justice movement has made much progress since it first began. At both the federal and state level, new policies and actions are being put in place to address the long-standing inequities in the ways pollution disproportionately impacts minorities and low-income populations. The policy-making process has become more inclusive with greater representation of people from diverse racial and ethnic backgrounds. While there is still more work ahead, the progress is something to be proud of as a nation showing the commitment to create a clean and healthy environment for all Americans.

Review/Discussion Questions

1. What is environmental justice?
2. Discuss the difference between equality, equity, and justice.
3. Discuss the evolution of the environmental justice movement. What are the key turning points in the movement?
4. What policies and laws can be used to enforce environmental justice?
5. What is your state doing to address environmental justice?

Resource

EJScreen Tool: https://ejscreen.epa.gov/mapper/

References

Agency for Toxic Substances and Disease Registry. (2021). *At a Glance: CDC Social Vulnerability Index (SVI)*. Retrieved on March 12, 2021 from www.atsdr.cdc.gov/placeandhealth/svi/at-a-glance_svi.html

Barnett, N. (2020). Regan's Record on EJ Won Him the Top EPA Spot. *The News & Observer*. December 2020. Retrieved on February 17, 2021 from www.newsobserver.com/opinion/article248011340.html

Bryant, B., and Mohai, P. (1992). Race, Poverty, and the Environment. *EPA Journal*. 18 (1): 8.

Bullard, R. (1990). *Dumping in Dixie: Race, Class, and Environmental Quality*. Boulder, CO: Westview Press.

Coye, M., and Lavelle, M. (1992). Unequal Protection. *National Law Journal*. 15 (3): S1–S2.

Farber, D., Eskidge, N., and Frickey, P. (1993). *Constitutional Law: Themes for the Constitution's Third Century*. St. Paul, MN: West Publishing Co. Appendix 1, 13.

Murphy-Greene, C. (2007). Environmental Justice: A Global Perspective. in *Handbook of Globalization and the Environment* (pp. 473–489). Eds. Thai, K., Rahm, D., Coggburn, J. New York, NY: Taylor and Francis, Inc.

Murphy-Greene, C. (2010). Agricultural Workers and Environmental Justice: An Assessment of the Federal Worker Protection Standards. in *Speaking Green with a Southern Accent: Exceptionalism and Environmental Innovation in the South* (pp. 95–114). Ed. Moriss, J. Lexington, MA: Lexington Press.

Murphy-Greene, C., and Leip, L. (2002). Assessing the Effectiveness of Executive Order 12898: Environmental Justice for All? *Public Administration Review.* 62 (6): 650–658.

Perls, H. (2021). *EPA Undermines Its Own Environmental Justice Programs*. Environmental and Energy Law Program, Harvard Law School. Retrieved on October 1, 2021 from https://eelp.law.harvard.edu/2020/11/epa-undermines-its-own-environmental-justice-programs/

Rush, B. (2019). "Rush Introduces Legislation Honoring" The Mother of Environmental Justice. *Hazel Johnson*. Retrieved on March 2, 2021 from https://rush.house.gov/media-center/press-releases/rush-introduces-legislation-honoring-the-mother-of-environmental-justice

State of North Carolina. (2021). *North Carolina Department of Environmental Quality Community Mapping System*. Retrieved on May 13, 2021 from https://deq.nc.gov/outreach-education/environmental-justice/deq-north-carolina-community-mapping-system

United Church of Christ. (1987). *Toxic Waste and Race in the United States*. The Commission for Racial Justice. p. xiii–xiv. New York: The Commission on Racial Justice.

US Department of Justice. (2021). *Title VI of the Civil Rights Act*. Retrieved on February 17, 2021 from www.justice.gov/crt/fcs/TitleVI-Overview

US Environmental Protection Agency. (2021a). *Learn about Environmental Justice*. Retrieved on October 1, 2021 from www.epa.gov/environmentaljustice/learn-about-environmental-justice.

US Environmental Protection Agency. (2021b). *Summary of Executive Order 12898: Federal Actions to Address Environmental Justice in Minority and Low-Income Populations*. Retrieved on October 2, 2021 from www.epa.gov/laws-regulations/summary-executive-order-12898-federal-actions-address-environmental-justice

White House. (2021). *White House Environmental Justice Advisory Council*. Retrieved on May 3, 2021 from www.epa.gov/environmentaljustice/white-house-environmental-justice-advisory-council.

2

CLIMATE JUSTICE AND VULNERABLE POPULATIONS

Celeste Murphy-Greene and Michael A. Brown

Introduction

According to the International Panel on Climate Change (IPCC), there is overwhelming evidence demonstrating human activity is impacting global climate (IPCC, 2021). Climate is the long-term trends in atmospheric conditions over decades, centuries, and longer (Robertson, 2021). Climate change refers to changes in the state of climate systems, which include temperature, precipitation, and wind (Robertson, 2021).

Climate change causes more frequent weather disasters, sea-level rise, extreme heat, droughts, poor air quality, and insect-related diseases. It is "a threat that magnifies other threats" (USC, 2020). While the direct impacts of climate change pose serious threats to Earth's ecosystem, the indirect impacts magnify threats to public health. As a result, climate change is now the top threat to global public health (USC, 2018). Additionally, according to the United Nations Security Council, in 2019 weather-related hazards displaced 24.9 million people in 140 countries (2021b). These social disruptions impact global security.

The impacts of climate change disproportionately impact the most vulnerable populations in society; the poor, elderly, and minorities (White-Newsome et al., 2018). As a result of the inequities of the impacts of climate change, this scientific phenomenon has become a social justice issue. The intersection of climate change and social justice is referred to as climate justice (Caney, 2020). This chapter focuses on climate justice by exploring the impacts of climate change on vulnerable communities in the United States and globally. Current US and international policies and strategies addressing climate change will be presented.

DOI: 10.4324/9781003186076-3

Global Climate Justice

In the 1980s and 1990s, the environmental justice movement gained strength and recognition in the United States, moving from a grassroots movement to a national issue. As the environmental justice movement earned attention in the United States, the US EPA, the United Nations, the IPCC, and scholars began focusing more research on the issue of climate justice as a global issue (IPCC, 2021; Murphy-Greene, 2007; United Nations, 2021a).

The IPCC was established in 1988 by the World Meteorological Organization (WMO) and the United Nations Environment Programme (UNEP) to provide policy makers regular assessments of the scientific basis of climate change, its impacts and future risks and options for adaption. The IPCC assessments are written by independent scientists who volunteer their time to contribute their research to the body of literature on climate change used by the IPCC. Within the IPCC there are three working groups: (1) The Physical Science Basis, (2) Impacts, Adaptation, and Vulnerability, and (3) Mitigation of Climate Change (IPCC, 2021). The IPCC is made up of 195 member countries.

In 2021, the IPCC issued its sixth assessment report. The report demonstrates the rapid warming temperatures over land and oceans. According to the IPCC (2021) report:

> Climate change is intensifying the water cycle. This brings more intense rainfall and associated flooding, as well as more intense drought in many regions.
>
> Climate change is affecting rainfall patterns. In high latitudes, precipitation is likely to increase, while it is projected to decrease over large parts of the subtropics. Changes to monsoon precipitation are expected, which will vary by region.
>
> Coastal areas will see continued sea level rise throughout the 21st century, contributing to more frequent and severe coastal flooding in low-lying areas and coastal erosion. Extreme sea level events that previously occurred once in 100 years could happen every year by the end of this century.
>
> Further warming will amplify permafrost thawing, and the loss of seasonal snow cover, melting of glaciers and ice sheets, and loss of summer Arctic sea ice.
>
> Changes to the ocean, including warming, more frequent marine heatwaves, ocean acidification, and reduced oxygen levels have been clearly linked to human influence. These changes affect both ocean ecosystems and the people that rely on them, and they will continue throughout at least the rest of this century.
>
> For cities, some aspects of climate change may be amplified, including heat (since urban areas are usually warmer than their surroundings), flooding from heavy precipitation events and sea level rise in coastal cities.
>
> *IPCC, 2021*

As the threat from climate change continues to increase globally, the impacts are felt more intensely by vulnerable populations throughout the world.

According to the United Nations Secretary-General Antonio Guterres, "Climate change is happening now and to all of us. No country or community is immune. And as always is the case, the poor, and vulnerable are the first to suffer and the worst hit" (Guterres, 2021). The United Nations' statement on climate change is as follows:

> The impacts of climate change will not be borne equally or fairly, between rich and poor, women and men, and older and younger generations. Consequently, there has been a growing focus on climate justice, which looks at the climate crisis through a human rights lens and on the belief that by working together we can create a better future for present and future generations.
>
> *United Nations, 2021a*

Thus, climate justice is an issue of growing importance to researchers and policy makers. In 2015, at the United Nations Climate Change Conference, world leaders signed the Paris Agreement (United Nations, 2021b). Today, there are 191 parties including 190 countries and the European Union.

The Agreement sets three long-term goals to guide all nations:

- substantially reduce global greenhouse gas emissions to limit the global temperature increase in this century to 2 degrees Celsius while pursuing efforts to limit the increase even further to 1.5 degrees;
- review countries' commitments every five years;
- provide financing to developing countries to mitigate climate change, strengthen resilience and enhance abilities to adapt to climate impacts.

United Nations, 2021b

As more research is conducted on the impacts of climate change, the impacts on the most vulnerable should be a priority.

To better understand climate justice, it is important to analyze the data showing that climate change is indeed occurring. Figure 2.1 illustrates the steadily increasing global temperatures of land and oceans from 1880 to 2020.

As the data reveals temperatures from the 1880s show an increase dating back to the 1940s with a steady and sharp upward trend in the late 1970s and the early 1980s (NOAA, 2021a). In 2020, the increase in temperature hit 1°C and 1.8°F. According to the National Oceanic and Atmospheric Administration:

- 2020 was the second-warmest year on record based on NOAA's temperature data, and land areas were record warm.

Global land and ocean
January–December temperature anomalies

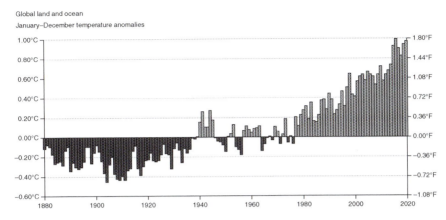

FIGURE 2.1 Global Land and Ocean: January–December Temperature Anomalies (NOAA, 2021a)

- Averaged across land and ocean, the 2020 surface temperature was 1.76°F (0.98°C) warmer than the 20th century average of 57.0°F (13.9°C) and 2.14°F (1.19°C) warmer than the pre-industrial period (1880–1900).
- Despite a late-year La Niña event that cooled a wide swath of the tropical Pacific Ocean, 2020 came just 0.04°F (0.02°C) shy of tying 2016 for warmest year on record.
- Earth's temperature has risen by 0.14°F (0.08°C) per decade since 1880, and the rate of warming over the past 40 years is more than twice that: 0.32°F (0.18°C) per decade since 1981.
- The 10 warmest years on record have occurred since 2005.
- From 1900 to 1980 a new temperature record was set on average every 13.5 years; from 1981 to 2019, a new record was set every 3 years (NOAA, 2021a).

The data is clear that Earth's temperature is rising at rates never experienced before. One might ask: What is driving these unprecedented temperature increases? The answer is anthropogenic or human caused changes to climate are documented in the increased levels of carbon released in the atmosphere (Robertson, 2021). A massive amount of ancient carbon has been stored or sequestered underground for millions of years in the form of decaying plants and other organic matter (Robertson, 2021). The extraction of this matter to use as fossil fuels has steadily increased. "Since the start of the industrial era the concentration of carbon in the atmosphere has risen more than 40%. The burning of fossil fuels is the main culprit; wood burning, farming deforestation, and cement production also contribute significant amounts" (Robertson, 2021, p. 94). Figure 2.2 illustrates the fluctuating levels of carbon in Earth's atmosphere within the last 800,000 years (NOAA, 2021b).

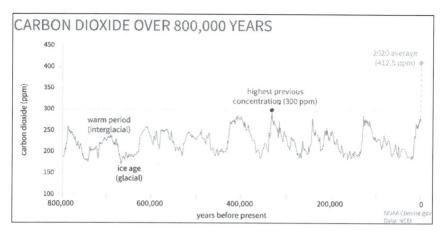

FIGURE 2.2 Carbon Dioxide over 800,000 Years

Figure 2.2 illustrates carbon dioxide levels never exceeded 300 parts per million (ppm) until recent times. At the end of the last ice age, carbon dioxide levels measured at 280 ppm. Today, it is close to 410 ppm. Ancient levels of carbon data are accessed through ice samples (Robertson, 2021). This data provides strong evidence of the linkages between increased carbon in the atmosphere and Earth's warming temperatures. If temperatures continue on this upward trajectory, the impacts will cause severe social disruptions, increase public health issues, and international conflicts (United Nations, 2021b).

According to the United Nations Security Council:

> Increasingly, the Council and other multilateral organizations stress climate actions as integral to peace in countries and regions, and as a basis for international security. In fragile countries in particular, governments often have limited resources to manage climate and other crises while helping vulnerable populations adapt to consequences such as drought and rising temperatures. In 2019, weather-related hazards displaced some 24.9 million people in 140 countries around the world, with climate change predicted to grow in force. Many women and girls face specific consequences, which the Council has recognized in its women, peace, and security agenda.
>
> *United Nations, 2021b*

Therefore, the issue of climate justice must be one where all countries in the global community understand the intersection of climate change, public health, and global security. Countries less equipped to deal with extreme weather, such as intense hurricanes, extended droughts, and rising sea-levels, are already experiencing mass migrations (Ulmer, 2021). Figure 2.3 presents temperature changes globally from 1901 to 2020 showing the regions around the world most vulnerable to climate change.

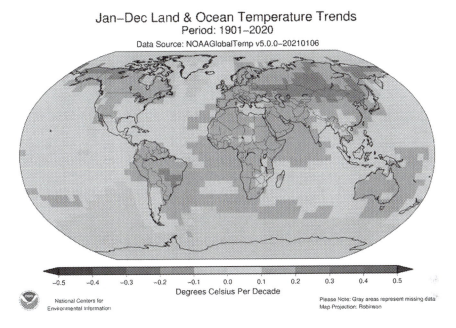

FIGURE 2.3 January–December Land and Ocean Temperature Trends, Period: 1901–2020

The darker areas depict the areas where climate change is currently having the most significant impact. Another index assessing a country's risk to climate change is the Global Climate Risk Index (Germanwatch, 2021). The Global Climate Risk Index is based on the extent countries have been impacted by weather related loss events such as floods, storms, and heat, human losses such as fatalities, and economic losses. The top ten countries with the greatest risk to climate change are: (1) Puerto Rico, (2) Myanmar, (3) Haiti, (4) Philippines, (5) Mozambique, (6) The Bahamas, (7) Bangladesh, (8) Pakistan, (9) Thailand, and (10) Nepal (Germanwatch, 2021). While this list does not cover all the countries most at risk, it gives policy makers and the public a better sense of where the most vulnerable populations at risk to climate change are located. It should be noted, several regions of Africa are at risk to climate change and did not make the top ten list. This chapter will now explore some of the countries most at risk to climate change.

CASES OF CLIMATE INJUSTICE: VULNERABLE REGIONS OF THE WORLD

Haiti

According to the World Bank, Haiti is the poorest country in the Latin American and Caribbean region and among the poorest countries in the world (World Bank, 2021). Due to long-term political instability, Haiti's social and economic development is hindered. The gross domestic product (GDP) per capita is $11,490 (in US dollars) and the country has a Human Development Index ranking of 170 out of 189 countries. In 2020, Haiti's poverty rate was 60% with two-thirds of the country's poor living in rural areas. Haiti is extremely vulnerable to natural disasters with more than 90% of the population at risk. In the last five years, Haiti has been hit by two major hurricanes. In 2016, Hurricane Matthew battered the south of Haiti, which was the most devastating disaster since the 2010 earthquake and in 2021 Hurricane Ida caused major damage. As a result of these natural disasters, many Haitians are without homes, electricity, jobs, and food, leading to displacement of thousands of people. In September 2021, reports of over 10,000 mostly Haitians attempted to migrate to the United States via Mexico only to be flown back to Haiti (BBC, 2021; Ulmer, 2021). These migration efforts come weeks after Hurricane Ida devastated Haiti. Haiti is an example of a country extremely vulnerable to climate change as it is prone to intense hurricanes, which magnify already existing social issues such as its high poverty rate, inadequate infrastructure, and unstable government.

Sub-Saharan Africa

Climate change manifests itself differently in different regions of the world. North Africa is predicted to experience a reduction in rainfall by the end of the 21st century, whereas the mountainous region of East Africa is predicted to experience increased rainfall (Bakhtsiyarava et al., 2018). Sub-Saharan Africa (SSA) is particularly vulnerable to climate change because of its low adaptive capacity and geographic characteristics (Bakhtsiyarava et al., 2018). Climate change affects human health through the changing patterns of seasonal disease, physical injuries from extreme weather events, and thermal stress (McMichael et al., 2006). Food availability is another important link between climate change and public health. "Undernutrition and poor child growth account for 11% of annual gross domestic product losses in Africa. In 2016, one third of the children in Africa experienced stunted growth" (Bakhtsiyarava et al., 2018, p. S145).

When examining agricultural practices in the countries of Kenya and Mali, it is evident that climate variability impacts farming practices and crop yield. Crop yield in turn impacts maternal nutrition, which affects children's birth weight. In Kenya, 6% of births were low birth weight (LBW) compared with 15% in Mali. Pastoralists in both countries experienced the highest LBW with 7% in Kenya and 20% in Mali. Farmers in both countries showed sensitivity to both positive (precipitation) and negative (increased temperature) effects of climate variability. The research indicates climate variability impacts food availability, which in turn impacts child health in communities with different agricultural practices. One factor complicating research in this area is 65% of births in SSA are not weighed. However, data does show a linkage between climate change and birth outcomes in Mali and Kenya. Thus, the intersection of climate change and public health is evident in Africa. Global public health focuses on equity and justice in health and within society. Global public health promotes social justice and should be seen as a common good. As countries most vulnerable to climate change experience more severe weather, the impacts on the most vulnerable will continue to increase.

Climate Change and Public Health: A California Case Study

The impact of climate change on public health is an issue of growing importance. When examining the impacts of climate change on those in the United States, Ganesh and Smith (2018) provide strong evidence of the impacts of climate change on California's San Joaquin Valley. This region of California is often referred to as "the nation's salad bowl" due to the fertile soil and the large variety of crops grown in this area. The large agricultural industry in the valley accounted for $47 billion in 2015. However, this region of California is in stark contrast to the socioeconomic levels of the rest of California. Hispanics make up 48.5% of the population in the San Joaquin Valley, approximately 30% of the population does not have a high school diploma, and one-fifth of the households in the region have incomes below the poverty level. Additionally, 84% of the population has limited English proficiency. California has been significantly hotter in the last several years with 2014 more than 3°F hotter compared with historical data from 1949–2005. The years 2012–2014 were the three hottest and driest on record. As temperatures have significantly increased in the region, there has been a significant decrease in precipitation and run-off.

The health-related impacts of climate change in the San Joaquin Valley are particularly striking in comparison to the rest of the state. From 2005–2010, heat-related emergency room visits averaged 17–25 per 100,000 compared with 11 per 100,000 for the state average. Since the main occupation of the region is agriculture, the rise in heat-related hospitalizations may be related to physical strain in combination with prolonged outdoor exposure to heat. Additionally, due to the combination of heat waves, changing weather patterns, and dust storms, the cases of Valley Fever (a disease caused by fungus found in the soil in California) increased by sixfold from 2000–2011 with 75% if the cases in the San Joaquin Valley.

In addition to the physical health impacts of climate change, Ganesh and Smith (2018) examine the impacts of climate change on mental health. The authors found that extreme heat caused mental health issues for farmers in drought-stricken areas. Another impact of climate change is solastalgia, a sense of desolation and loss of identity when one's home and environment become uninhabitable.

In order to address the unequal impacts of climate change, California has a two-pronged approach: mitigation and adaptation. Mitigation involves taking steps to reduce the impacts of climate change by cutting greenhouse gasses (GHGs) with the Global Warming Solutions Act (GWSA) of 2006. The GWSA requires a reduction in GHG emissions to 40% below 1990 levels by 2030 (State of California, 2006). California currently uses a cap-and-trade system to reduce GHGs.

The cap and trade approach works by the state setting a cap on emissions for companies. Companies that cut their emissions below the set cap can earn credits and sell them on the market or bank them. California's cap and trade policy has generated funds that the state uses on projects to reduce GHG emissions. Additionally, in 2012 the state passed SB 535, which requires 25% of the monies from the GHG fund to be spent on projects that benefit disadvantages communities with 10% of the funds spent of specific projects located within these disadvantaged communities.

Adaptation is the second part of California's climate change strategy. California's adaptation plan addresses the following areas: extreme heat, wildfire, drought, floods, and sea-level rise. The key points of the plan include the following:

> 1) Strengthen protections for climate vulnerable communities; 2) Protect public health and safety in the event of climate disasters; 3) Reduce climate risks to California's economy; 4) Help nature adapt to climate change, and accelerate nature-based solutions, 5) Make decisions based on best available climate science, 6) Leverage resources for climate action through partnerships and collaboration.
>
> *State of California, 2021*

This plan is required by California law to be updated every three years. Both California's mitigation and adaptation plans include a climate justice approach by including protections and/or resources for disadvantaged and vulnerable communities.

Climate Change and the Elderly

One largely overlooked population at risk to the impacts of climate change are the elderly. Elderly are those ages 65 and older. According to Filberto et al. (2008), elderly are more at risk to the impacts of climate change, such as extreme heat, wind, and excess precipitation, due to their lower adaptive capacity as a result of decreased mobility resulting from age, changes in physiology, and restricted access to resources. The impacts of Hurricane Ida in September of 2021 in Louisiana illustrate how severe weather can affect elderly populations (Cusick & Knowles, 2021). As a result of the hurricane, more than 800 residents from 7 nursing home facilities were brought to a warehouse in Independence, Louisiana. The conditions at the warehouse were not suitable for this vulnerable population with reports of putrid smells of urine and people packed on mattresses. As a result of the unsuitable conditions, seven residents died at the warehouse. This case highlights the risk severe weather poses to elder populations and the need for emergency management plans to include plans for evacuating elderly populations in the face of extreme weather. The issue of emergency management and at risk populations will be explored in greater detail later in this book.

In addition to hurricanes, increased heat waves is another factor impacting the elderly. According to Kaltsatou et al. (2018), heat waves cause thousands of deaths in elderly populations across the globe each year. One of the most deadly heat waves occurred in 2003 with 13,778 deaths in Italy's elderly population aged 75 years and older. This 12 day heat wave impacted 21 regions of Italy, where the number of deaths among 75 years and older increased by 21.3% in 2003 compared with 2002. Also in 2003, China lost 2,283 elderly due to heat-related factors. The authors also found elderly women in Spain had a higher mortality rate than men. Factors such as socioeconomic status were found to play a role in the higher mortality rate for these women. It was also found that women who lived alone had a higher mortality rate compared to men. In response to Europe's heat waves, heat protection strategies have been implemented in England showing positive results for the elderly populations (Kaltsatou et al., 2018). In 2013, a heat wave lasted from June 1 to September 15 with a significant reduction in deaths compared to previous heat waves.

According to Varquez et al. (2020), extreme heat in urban areas causes the creation of Urban Heat Islands (UHIs), which pose increased threats to elderly populations. When exploring the projected heat increases in Jakarta, Indonesia, the researchers found

> a 2050s projected increase by 12 to 15 times of 2010s heat-related elderly mortality count. This increase is closely proportional to the increase in the estimated elderly population between the 2010s and 2050s which is by a factor of 9 to 10.
>
> *Varquesz et al., 2020*

The health impacts of UHIs on the elderly and the general population are an issue of growing concern globally and in the United States. This chapter will now explore UHIs in greater detail.

Urban Heat Islands: A Public Health Threat

Studies have shown urban areas have increased temperatures compared to surrounding rural and/or suburban areas (Dang et al., 2018; Wilson, 2020). The result is the creation of UHIs. The main cause of the increased temperature in urban areas is a lack of green space and the predominance of impermeable surfaces such as concrete and asphalt which radiate heat from the sun. According to the US Environmental Protection Agency, on average, surface temperatures in developed areas can range from 18°F to 27°F hotter during the day and from 9°F to 18°F warmer at night than in rural areas (US Environmental Protection Agency, 2008). According to the Center for Disease Control (CDC), it is estimated in the US 600 people are killed each year due to extreme heat (Wilson, 2020). These numbers are much lower in comparison to the previously discussed number of heat-related deaths in Europe and China, but are still cause for concern. When examining the demographic breakdown of those most impacted by urban heat, a 2004 report by the Congressional Black Caucus found the negative consequences of climate change, including heat-related deaths and illnesses, are likely to disproportionately impact African Americans living in cities in the United States. Wilson (2020) argues historical practices of discrimination and disinvestment, such as redlining, have contributed to the current landscape of urban heat and its impact on vulnerable populations. The historical practice of redlining will now be discussed in greater detail.

The Legacy of Redlining in the United States: Impact on Urban Areas

Palm and Corbridge defined redlining as "geographical discrimination used in financial lending to keep persons of color from purchasing homes or securing a mortgage in predominantly White residential areas" (1982, p. 341; Dingemans, 1979; Szto, 2013). Redlining practices were used in cities throughout the United States until the 1960s. Figure 2.4 shows a "Residential Security Map" of Richmond, Virginia created by the city's Department of Public Works. Sections of the city are color coded to depict financially risky areas and financially safe areas.

The practice of redlining was not restricted to securing a mortgage. There is insurance redlining and reverse redlining. Insurance redlining is the refusal to insure property for a specific group thereby inhibiting them from being able to purchase property (Plitt & Maldonado, 2008). Reverse redlining is the practice of providing inferior financial and/or unfair credit products with targeted

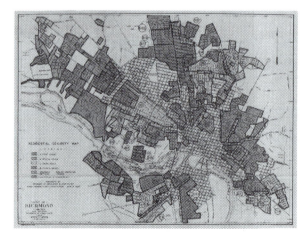

FIGURE 2.4 City of Richmond Residential Security Map

Source: Nelson and Ayers (2021).

discrimination toward specific groups (Szto, 2013). In the 1930s, the Home Owners Loan Corporation (HOLC) developed maps specifically designed to ensure the separation and continued discriminatory practice of redlining. Fishback et al. (2020) argued that the Federal Housing Administration (FHA) acted as a partner in this discriminatory practice. Kimble argues the FHA "played a more direct role in redlining" (2018, p. 399).

It was not until the Fair Housing Act of 1964 was enacted to provide constitutional restraints in the United States with regards to ensuring fair housing that at least some action by the federal government to deal with housing discrimination was evident (CRS, 2016). Steil et al.'s (2018) study presented evidence of historical disparities and unfair lending practices targeting Latinx and African American borrowers for decades. In Baltimore, Rugh et al.'s (2015, p. 2), research posited that African Americans and Latinx borrowers paid 5% more on their loans than Whites despite possessing less income. Contrary to some literature failing to transparently address the harmful practice of redlining, most empirical literature indisputably resembles the findings by Steil et al. (2018) and Nardone et al. (2020), which revealed that in major cities, e.g., Atlanta, Chicago, New York, and Miami, redlining is also responsible for health inequities directly connected to spatial systemic discrimination (p. 109).

The practice of redlining combined with social and environmental inequity produces cascading threats and hazardous conditions, such as increased flooding and crisis level in UHIs for the most vulnerable citizens in our communities (Margulis, 1997; Saverino et al., 2021; Zenou & Boccard, 1999). For example, exposure from UHI effect presents an imminent and present danger to the most underserved and marginalized in our cities (Saverino et al., 2021). UHI effect is the result of human-made activities (e.g., over building, poor urban design, lack of mitigation, negligent zoning) that negatively affects and disrupts the routinization of societal norms and daily activities because of increased heat emanating from the atmospheric canopy layer over urban areas (Giannaros et al., 2014, p. 347; Saverino et al., 2021). It is well documented that UHI is a result of over urbanization, and such phenomena are not as prevalent in rural areas with data provided from thermal remote sensing (Voogt & Oke, 2003).

The threat from UHIs affects minorities in a significantly disproportionate manner and is another byproduct of racial zoning and redlining, which restrict persons of color from living in more hospitable spatial settings (p. 1). In Richmond, Virginia most Blacks live on the East side of the city which is more urban and Whites in the suburban West End. The higher median income and lower levels of poverty are in the White residential areas. According to Saverino et al., though Blacks made up 48% of the Richmond population in 2018 they represented 65% of those impoverished within the city (2021). This is important because socioeconomic status and race are factors that determine access to financing, education, and available residential settings. In 2016, data from the Multi-Resolution Land Characteristics Consortium National Land Cover Database (NLCD) showed

77.2% of Richmond's developed surface shows elevated temperatures compared to suburban areas and retains heat (p. 4).

Health Issues Caused by Chronic Exposure to Heat

There are numerous health issues caused and manifested within communities of color because of redlining and the UHI effect. Collin et al.'s (2021) study noted the prevalence of breast cancer in Latinx and Blacks. Their study noted a 60% increase in breast cancer mortality with persons residing in areas considered regressive in lending practices and considered redlined (p. 1). The quantitative study by Nardone et al. (2020) presented results on health-related problems in persons of color from nine major cities that supported a correlation between ethnicity and racial health disparities in what they refer to as spatially patterned neighborhoods of color. Likewise, Saverino et al. argued that the increase in land temperature under the urban canopy of UHIs affects minorities disproportionately because they lack central air conditioning in their dwellings and access to healthcare (2021). Hoffman et al. (2020) documented increased national land temperature of 2.6% warmer than non-redlined urban areas that contributed to health problems and stated, "extreme heat is the leading cause of summer-time morbidity and has specific impacts on those communities with pre-existing health conditions (e.g., chronic obstructive pulmonary disease, asthma, cardio-vascular disease, etc.), limited access to resources, and the elderly" (p. 1.; Hess et al., 2014).

Community-Based Resilience Strategies to Address Climate Change

Urban Heat Management is a new term referring to the ongoing strategy of municipal governments to physically reduce the intensity and duration of heat exposure, both during and outside of periods of extreme heat (Wilson, 2020). Wilson encourages urban planners and municipal government to use an equity lens in resilience planning. Linking current disparities in heat exposure to past policies and actions brings a procedural and recognitional equity lens to bear and strongly makes the case for planning interventions to redress long-standing injustices (Meerow et al., 2019). Incorporating an equity lens into resilience planning by state and local government is a growing practice. According to Meerow et al. (2019), resilience at the local level involves cities accepting disruptions and change as inevitable and focusing on enhancing the ability of the built environment, institutions, and communities to cope with these changes and adapt. Meerow et al. argue current resiliency levels of communities are highly unequal, with lower income and minority communities not equally prepared to cope with environmental disruptions such as heat waves and hurricanes. Therefore, when focusing on resiliency with an equity lens, the goal is for all community members to be prepared for the inevitable environmental disruption.

In order to help all community members achieve social equity and justice in resilience planning, Meerow et al. (2019) present a three-part framework. This framework includes procedural, recognition, and distributional equity dimensions (Meerow et al., 2019). As was discussed in the previous chapter, procedural equity focuses on equitable participation in the decision-making processes. This includes a focus on participation in plan development, governance, and outreach to marginalized groups. Recognitional equity focuses on acknowledgment and respect of different groups, recognizing a group's history and needs. Distributional equity focuses on the equitable distribution of goods, services, and opportunities. This includes goods, such as infrastructure and environmental amenities. In response to the need to address equity and justice issues in resilience planning, localities across the United States have integrated equity and justice into their resilience plans.

Tackling Climate Change at the Local Level: The Case of Richmond, VA

The City of Richmond, Virginia is an example of a municipality working to address climate justice at the local level with its justice focused climate action plan RVAgreen2050. The RVAgreen2050 plan uses an equity and justice lens working to identify vulnerable communities at high risk to the impacts of climate change such as high precipitation, causing recurrent flooding, and extreme heat in urban areas. Richmond's resilience plan, like California's plan discussed previously in this chapter, is a two-pronged approach focusing on mitigation and adaption. To help mitigate the impacts of climate change and adapt to those changes "Richmond's equity centered climate action plan seeks to reduce greenhouse gas emissions by 45% by 2030, achieve zero emissions by 2050, and help communities adapt to Richmond's climate impacts of extreme heat, precipitation, and flooding" (City of Richmond, 2021). In addition to focusing on both mitigation of the causes of climate change and adaption to those ongoing changes, Richmond's plan addresses historic injustices. The plan states:

> Due to historic and institutional racism, people of color are more likely to live in more marginal and exposed areas that are more susceptible to climate impacts. For these reasons, it is critical that the City of Richmond's efforts to address climate change are carried out in a way that is inclusive and protects our most vulnerable communities.
>
> *City of Richmond, 2021*

Using an equity and justice lens, the RVAgreen2050 plan involves partnerships with local universities, nonprofits, and government agencies. The University

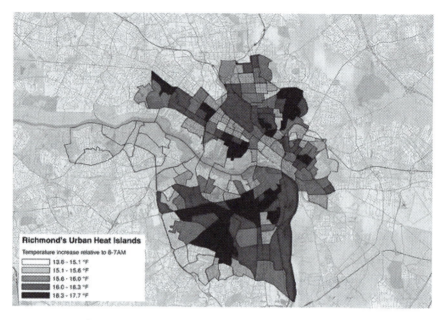

FIGURE 2.5 Richmond's Urban Heat Islands

of Richmond's Mapping Inequality Project provides maps of redlined communities, and Virginia Museum of Science provides the expertise in helping identify Richmond's Urban Heath Islands. Figure 2.5 illustrates the temperature variations throughout the city showing Richmond's UHI's using a Heat Vulnerability Index.

The factors included in the Heat Vulnerability Index include the following:

- Poverty
- Age (children and elderly)
- Disability
- Working outdoors
- Vehicle access
- Housing status
- Housing cost burden
- Lack of central air conditioning
- Health conditions (COPD, heart disease, high blood pressure, asthma, diabetes, kidney disease, obesity)

In order to address the issue of UHIs, the City of Richmond is working with local nonprofit organizations and universities. In summer of 2017, the City of Richmond partnered with the Science Museum of Virginia, Virginia Commonwealth University, University of Richmond, and Groundwork RVA to enhance awareness and understanding of the urban heat burden in Richmond and develop ways to reduce UHI-related impacts (City of Richmond, 2021).

Groundwork RVA is a local nonprofit in Richmond working to address the issues of climate justice within the community by making Richmond greener, more sustainable, and more equitable. Through the support of the US Environmental Protection Agency, the National Park Service, the City of Richmond, and Groundwork USA, this community-based organization involves youth in leadership and programs to increase green space and green infrastructure to enhance neighborhood climate resilience. Green infrastructure is defined as

> a strategically planned and managed network of wilderness, parks, greenways, conservation easements, and working lands conservation value that supports native species, maintains ecological processes, sustains air and water resources, and contributes to the health and quality of life for America's communities and people.
>
> *Benedict and McMahon, 2006*

Through Groundwork's Green Team, they involve at risk recent high school graduates creating sustainable landscapes and community greening projects. This helps youth build work experience and contribute to the health and sustainability of their community.

Richmond is also encouraging residents to take steps to address climate change and reduce urban heat using the following steps:

- Plant trees or care for trees in neighborhoods
- Install a vegetated or green roof
- Create a green space on vacant land or help maintain an existing green space
- Install permeable surfaces on roadways, sidewalks, parking lots, and alleys

Increasing the urban tree canopy and green space with green infrastructure and reducing impermeable surfaces that radiate heat have shown to have a positive impact on reducing UHIs and flooding caused by climate change. The inclusion of more green infrastructure using native plants helps communities to become more resilient to extreme weather and is visually appealing. Thus far, this chapter has reviewed international, state (California), and local (Richmond) policies to address climate justice. Now the chapter will focus on what the US federal government is doing to address climate justice.

Federal Actions to Address Climate Justice

In an effort to address the issue of climate change, the Biden Administration, assuming office in January 2021, has taken several bold steps. The first major step was rejoining the Paris Agreement. The Paris Agreement, as discussed previously in this chapter, sets long-term international goals to address climate change by reducing GHGs. It is important to note, the United States originally joined the Paris Agreement in 2015, but the Trump Administration withdrew the United States from the agreement shortly after taking office in 2017. Building on the three goals of the Paris Agreement, on January 27, 2021 President Joe Biden signed Executive Order (EO) 14008: Tackling Climate Change at Home and Abroad (White House, 2021a). EO 14008 takes bold steps to address climate change domestically and abroad. The first part of the two-part plan is titled "Putting the Climate Crisis at the Center of U.S. Foreign Policy and National Security." The second part is titled "Taking a Government Wide Approach to the Climate Crisis" focusing on domestic efforts to address climate change. Each section of the two-part plan will now be discussed.

Putting climate change at the center of the US foreign policy and national security is a bold move. In this effort, EO 14008 calls for the creation of a newly appointed Special Presidential Envoy for Climate, to elevate the issue of climate change and underscore the administration's commitment toward addressing this important issue. Additionally, the EO calls for a focus on a climate finance plan to assist developing countries implement emissions reduction plans and build resilience against the impacts of climate change. A third part of the plan calls for leading the US national security officials, including the Secretaries of Defense and Homeland Security and the Joint Chiefs of Staff to consider the security implications of climate change.

The second part of the Biden climate action plan has a domestic focus. First, the plan calls for the creation of a White House Office of Domestic Climate Policy to lead the coordination of domestic climate policy efforts. The EO also creates the National Climate Task Force (NCTF), chaired by the National Climate Advisor. The NCTF's mission is to facilitate the organization and deployment of a government wide approach to combat the climate crisis. The NCTF consists of the heads of federal agencies and departments. EO 14008 also provides for the creation of a Civilian Climate Corps Initiative (CCCI) to mobilize the next generation of conservation and resilient workers. The CCCI can be viewed as a domestic climate-focused Peace Corps. The EO also promotes a federal clean electricity and vehicle procurement strategy, with the goal of a carbon pollution free electricity sector by 2035. The promotion of renewable energy on public lands and in offshore waters is also a key component. The plan also focuses on the federal investment in infrastructure reduces climate pollution and requires federal permitting decisions consider the effects of GHG emissions and climate change. The role of agriculture and forestry is another key component where the plan calls on the Secretary of Agriculture to gather input from tribes, farmers, ranchers, forest owners, conservation groups, firefighters, and other stakeholders to encourage the voluntary adoption of climate-smart practices that result in reduces wildfires and result in measurable carbon reductions and sequestration. Carbon sequestration through regenerative agriculture is a growing practice in the United States. This low-impact farming practice draws down carbon from the atmosphere and sequesters it in the soil while also promoting soil health, using less fertilizer, and water (Morgan et al., 2010).

The Justice40 Initiative is a key part of EO 14008, focusing on vulnerable populations (White House, 2021b). Justice40 is a whole-of-government effort to ensure federal agencies work in coordination with states and local communities to ensure at least 40% of the overall benefits from federal investments in climate change and clean energy be allocated to disadvantaged communities (White House, 2021b). Justice40 investments in clean energy and energy efficiency, clean transit, affordable and sustainable housing, workforce development and training, remediation and reduction of legacy pollution, and development of critical clean water infrastructure. Legacy pollutants are contaminants left in the environment long after the polluters discharging them are no longer emitting them, such as an old industry that has since left the site.

Finally, EO 14008 directly addresses environmental justice through several initiatives. First, it recommends the Justice Department establish an Office of Environmental Justice to coordinate environmental justice efforts throughout the agency. Second, it establishes the Office of Climate Change and Health Equity to address the impacts of climate change on minorities and low-income populations. Third, the EO establishes the Interagency Working Group to decrease risk of climate change to children, the elderly, people with disabilities, and the vulnerable. Finally, the EO establishes the creation of an Environmental Justice Scorecard detailing agency environmental justice performance measures. The Biden Administration has outlined bold measures to address climate change both domestically and abroad. These actions are far reaching and include a strong focus on environmental justice as the impacts of climate change are greatest on the most vulnerable members of society.

Conclusion

This chapter has provided an in depth look at the far-reaching impacts of climate change on vulnerable populations in the United States and globally. A strong case has been made for the causes of climate change and the impact GHGs, such as carbon dioxide, are having on global temperatures. The evidence is clear, climate change is a threat to public health and national security. As global temperatures have rapidly increased in recent times, the impacts have disproportionately burdened the most vulnerable populations in the United States and globally. Those most impacted by climate change are the least equipped socially, economically, and politically to cope with the challenges of extreme heat, increased precipitation, wildfires, droughts, and strong winds.

Climate justice addresses the inequities of climate change by viewing resilience planning with an equity and justice lens. Resilience policies and actions at the international, federal, state, and local level have been presented. To address current inequities, resilience planning must involve recognition of current inequities and historic factors contributing to these inequities. The historic practice of redlining was explored in relation to the impacts of UHIs on minority populations. Public recognition and acknowledgment of previous discriminatory practices which magnify the current impacts of climate change are important to building trust with community members. Involving community members in strategies to enhance resiliency such as incorporating green infrastructure into urban areas helps strengthen communities' resilience and builds work experience for at risk individuals. Resilient communities with strong social, economic, and political structures are better able to cope with challenging environmental conditions. Therefore, to achieve climate justice, policy makers and communities must strive to implement resilience strategies that include a focus on the most vulnerable members of society.

Review/Discussion Questions

1. Define climate justice.
2. What is the Paris Agreement? Identify three long-term goals of this agreement.
3. What is redlining? Discuss how the impacts of redlining relate to UHIs?
4. Discuss a federal, state, or local policy addressing climate change. How does the policy incorporate resilience planning?

References

Bakhtsiyarava, M. et al. (2018). Climate, Birth Weight, and Agricultural Livelihoods in Kenya and Mali. *American Journal of Public Health*, *18*(52): 145–151.

BBC News. (2021, September 20). *Migrants in Texas: U.S. Flies Haitian Migrants Back Home from Border*. Retrieved on September 22, 2021 from www.bbc.com/news/world-us-canada-58620147.

Benedict, M., & McMahon, E. (2006). *Green Infrastructure: Linking Landscapes and Communities*. Washington, DC: Island Press.

Caney, S. (2020). "Climate Justice", *The Stanford Encyclopedia of Philosophy* (Summer 2020 Edition), E. N. Zalta (ed.). Retrieved on September 20, 2021 from https://plato.stanford.edu/archives/sum2020/entries/justice-climate/.

City of Richmond. (2021). *RVAgreen2050*. Retrieved on September 29, 2021 from www.rvagreen2050.com/extremeheat.

Collin, L. J., Gaglioti, A. H., Beyer, K. M., Zhou, Y., Moore, M. A., Nash, R., Switchenko, J. M., Miller-Kleinhenz, J. M., Ward, K. C., & McCullough, L. E. (2021). Neighborhood-level Redlining and Lending Bias are Associated with Breast Cancer Mortality in a Large and Diverse Metropolitan Area. *Cancer Epidemiology Biomarkers Preview*, *30*(1): 53–60. doi:10.1158/1055-9965.EPI-20-1038.

Congressional Report Services (CRS). (2016). The fair housing act (FHA): A legal overview. Retrieved from https://crsreports.congress.gov/product/pdf/RL/95-710/23

Cusick, A., & Knowles, H. (2021, September 5). "Families Scramble to Find Elderly Nursing Home Patients Taken to Warehouse Ahead of Ida", *Washington Post*. Retrieved on September 9, 2021 from www.washingtonpost.com/nation/2021/09/05/louisiana-ida-nursing-homes-closed/.

Dang et al. (2018). Green Space and Deaths Attributed to the Urban Heat Island: Effect in Ho Chi Minh City. *American Journal of Public Health, 108*: S137–S143.

Dingemans, D. (1979). Redlining and Mortgage Lending in Sacramento. *Association of American Geographers, 59*, 225–239.

Environmental Protection Agency. (2021). *Climate Change and Social Vulnerability in the U.S.: A Focus on Six Impacts.* Retrieved on September 19, 2021 from www.epa.gov/cira/social-vulnerability-report.

Filberto, D. et al. (2008). Older People and Climate Change: Vulnerability and Health Effects. *Generations, 33*(4): 19–25.

Fishback, P.V., LaVoice, J., Shertzer, A., & Walsh, R. (2020). The HOLC Maps: How Race and Influenced Real Estate Professional's Evaluation of Lending Risk in the 1930s. Retrieved from www.nber.org/system/files/working_papers/w28146/w28146.pdf

Ganesh, C. & Smith, J. (2018). Climate Change, Public Health, and Policy: A California Case Study. *American Journal of Public Health, 108*: S114–S119.

Germanwatch. (2021). *Global Climate Risk Index 2021.* Retrieved on September 27, 2021 from www.germanwatch.org/en/suche?search_api_fulltext=climate%20risk%20index%202021.

Giannaros, T. M, Melas, D., Daglis, I. A., & Keramitsoglou, I. (2014). Development of an Operational Modelling System for Urban Heat Islands: An Application to Athens, Greece. *Natural Hazards and Earth System Sciences, 14*: 347–358.

Guterres, A. (2021). *United Nations Sustainable Development Goals: Climate Justice.* Retrieved on September 22, 2021 from www.un.org/sustainabledevelopment/blog/2019/05/climate-justice/.

Hess, J. J., Eidson, M., Tlumak, J. E.; Raab, K. K., & George, L. (2014). An Evidence-based Public Health Approach to Climate Change Adaptation. *Environmental Health Perspective, 122*: 1177–1186.

Hoffman, J. S., Shandas, V., & Pendleton, N. (2020). The Effects of Historical Housing Policies on Resident Exposure to Intra-Urban Heat: A Study of 108 US Urban Areas. *Climate, 8*(12): 1–15.

International Panel on Climate Change. (2021). *Climate Change 2021: The Physical Science Basis.* Sixth Assessment Report. Retrieved on September 20, 2021 from www.ipcc.ch/assessment-report/ar6/.

Kaltsatou, A., Kenny, G., & Flouris, A. (2018). The Impact of Heat Waves on Mortality among Elderly: A Mini Systematic Review. *Geriatric Medicine and Gerontology, 4*(3): 1–9.

Kimble, J. (2018, December). Insuring Inequality: The role of the Federal Housing Administration in the urban ghettoization of African Americans. Retrieved from www.cambridge.org/core/journals/law-and-social-inquiry/article/abs/insuring-inequality-the-role-of-the-federal-housing-administration-in-the-urban-ghettoization-of-african-americans/BA9383566D7714FE48812857AEF0656B#

Margulis, H. L. (1997). Predicting the Growth and Filtering of At-risk Housing: Structure Ageing, Poverty and Redlining. *Urban Studies, 35*(8): 1231–1259.

McMichael, A. J., Woodruff, R. E., & Halles, S. (2006). Climate Change and Human Health: Present and Future Risks. *Lancet, 367*(9513): 859–869.

Meerow, S., Pajaouhesh, P., & Miller, T. (2019). Social Equity in Urban Resilience Planning. *Local Environment, 24*(9): 793–808.

Morgan, J., Follett, R., Allen Jr, L., Del Grosso, S., Derner, J., Dijkstra, F., Franzluebbers, A., Fry, R., Paustian, K., & Schoeneberger, M. (2010). Carbon Sequestration in Agricultural Lands of the U.S. *Journal of Water and Conservation, 65*(1): 6A–13A.

Murphy-Greene, C. (2007). Environmental Justice: A Global Perspective. In *Handbook of Globalization and the Environment*. Ed. Thai, K., Rahm, D. Goggburn, J. New York: Taylor and Francis. 473–489.

Nardone, A., Chiang, J., & Corburn, J. (2020). Historic Redlining and Urban Health Today in U.S. Cities. *Environmental Justice, 13*(4): 109–119.

National Oceanic and Atmospheric Administration. (2021a). *National Center for Environmental Information*. Annual 2020 Global Climate Report. Retrieved on September 22, 2021 from www.ncdov/sotc/global/202013#gtemp.

National Oceanic and Atmospheric Administration. (2021b). *Climate Change: Atmospheric Carbon Dioxide*. Retrieved on September 25, 2021 from https://climate.gov/news-featu res/understanding-climate/climate-change-atmospheric-carbon-dioxide.

Nelson, R., & Ayers, E. (2021). *Mapping Inequality*. Retrieved on September 29, 2021 from https://dsl.richmond.edu/panorama/redlining/#loc=11/36.914/-76.527&city=norf olk-va&text=downloads.

Palm, R., & Corbridge, J. (1982). The Unintended Impacts of Anti-redlining Legislation. *Journal of Environmental Systems, 12*(4): 341–350.

Plitt, S., & Maldonado, D. (2008). Prohibiting De Facto Insurance Redlining: Will Hurricane Katrina Draw a Discriminatory Redline in the Gulf Coast Sands Prohibiting Access to Home Ownership?, *Washington and Lee Journal of Civil Rights and Social Justice, 14*(2), 3: 198–254.

Robertson, M. (2021). *Sustainability Principles and Practice*. New York, NY: Routledge.

Rugh, J. S., Albright, L., & Massey, D. S. (2015). Race, Space, and Cumulative Disadvantage: A Case Study of the Subprime Lending Collapse. *Social Problems, 62*:186–218.

Saverino, K. C., Routman, E., Lookingbill, T. R., Eanes, A. E., Hoffman, J. S., & Bao, R. (2021). Thermal Inequity in Richmond, VA: The Effect of an Unjust Evolution of the Urban Landscape on Urban Heat Islands. *Sustainability, 13*(1511): 1–18.

State of California. (2006). *SB-535 California Global Warming Solutions Act of 2006: Greenhouse Gas Reduction Fund (2011-2102)*. Health and Safety Code.

State of California. (2021). *State Adaption Strategy: Building Resilience and Reducing Risk*. Retrieved on September 25, 2021 from http://opr.ca.gov/meetings/tac/2021-03-26/ docs/20210326-Item5_StateAdaptationStrategy.pdf.

Steil, S. P., Albright, L., Rugh, J. S., & Massey, D. S. (2018). The Social Structure of Mortgage Discrimination. *Housing Studies, 33*(5): 759–776.

Szto, M. (2013). Real Estate Agents as Agents of Social Change: Redlining, Reverse Eedlining, and Greenlining. *Seattle Journal for Social Justice, 12*(1) 2: 1–60.

Ulmer, A. (2021, September 18). *Over 10,000 Mostly Haitian Migrants Sleeping Under Texas Bridge, More Expected*. Reuters. Retrieved on September 22, 2021 from www.reuters. com/world/us/over-10000-mostly-haitian-migrants-sleeping-under-texas-bridge- more-expected-2021-09-17/.

United Nations. (2021a). *Sustainable Development Goals: Climate Justice*. Retrieved on September 22, 2021 from www.un.org/sustainabledevelopment/blog/2019/05/ climate-justice/

United Nations. (2021b). *The Paris Agreement*. Retrieved on September 30, 2021 from www.un.org/en/climatechange/paris-agreement.

United Nations. (2021c). *Security Council Open Debate on Climate and Security*. Retrieved on September 22, 2021 from www.un.org/en/climatechange/security-council-open- debate-climate-and-security-0.

University of Southern California. (2018). *How Climate Change Affects Public Health*. Keck School of Medicine. Retrieved on September 19, 2021 from https://mphdegree.usc. edu/blog/how-climate-change-affects-public-health/.

University of Southern California. (2020). *3 Global Public Health Threats*. Keck School of Medicine. Retrieved on September 19, 2021 from https://mphdegree.usc.edu/blog/3-global-public-health-threats/.

US Environmental Protection Agency. (2008). "Urban Heat Island Basics", *Reducing Urban Heat Islands: Compendium of Strategies* (pp. 1–22). Retrieved on September 28, 2021 from www.epa.gov/heat-islands/heatisland-compendium.

Varquez, A., Darmanto, N., Honda, Y., Ihara, T., & Kanda, M. (2020). Future Increase in Elderly with Heat-Related Mortality of a Rapidly Growing Asian City. *Scientific Reports*, *9304*: 1–9.

Voogt, J. A., & Oke, T. R. (2003). Thermal Remote Sensing of Urban Climates. *Remote Sensing of Environment*, *86*: 370–384.

White House. (2021a). *Executive Order 14008: Tackling the Climate Crisis at Home and Abroad*. Retrieved on September 30, 2021 from www.whitehouse.gov/briefing-room/presidential-actions/2021/01/27/executive-order-on-tackling-the-climate-crisis-at-home-and-abroad/.

White House. (2021b). *The Justice40 Initiative*. The Path to Achieving Justice40. Retrieved on September 20, 2021 from www.whitehouse.gov/omb/briefing-room/2021/07/20/the-path-to-achieving-justice40/.

White-Newsome, J., Meadows, P. & Kabel, C. (2018). Bridging Climate, Health, and Equity: A Growing Imperative. *American Journal of Public Health Perspectives*, Supplement 2; 108: S72–S73.

Wilson, B. (2020). Urban Heat Management and the Legacy of Redlining. *Journal of the American Planning Association*, 86(4): 443–457.

World Bank. (2021). *The World Bank in Haiti*. Retrieved on September 23, 2021 from www.worldbank.org/en/country/haiti/overview.

Zenou, Y., & Boccard, N. (1999). Racial Discrimination and Redlining Cities. CORE Discussion Papers, 13. Retrieved from http://hdl.handle.net/2078.1/4025.

3

COVID-19

Addressing Health Equity in the United States

Celeste Murphy-Greene and Michael A. Brown

Introduction

On March 11, 2020, the World Health Organization declared COVID-19 a pandemic (WHO, 2021). Since that time, communities across the globe have experienced multiple waves of rising cases and deaths. As of November 3, 2021, the COVID-19-induced pandemic has taken the lives of 749,064 individuals in the United States and over 5 million globally (Johns Hopkins University, 2021). The pandemic is one of the greatest threats to global public health in modern times and has disproportionately impacted minorities in the United States (Sheahan & Freiman, 2020; Tai et al., 2021). This chapter explores the issue of health equity by examining the disparate impacts of COVID-19 on communities of color throughout the United States. Some of the questions that will be addressed are: (1) How are populations in the United States impacted by COVID-19? (2) What racial/ethnic disparities are apparent? and (3) What strategies can be used to help communities at high risk effectively deal with COVID-19? The issue of vaccine hesitancy will also be explored. Finally, strategies to address health inequities and help build more resilient and sustainable communities in the wake of the pandemic will be presented.

Navigating Through a Pandemic: Addressing Health Inequities

After raging throughout the entire global community for a year and a half, the pandemic is currently in its second major wave in the United States. The COVID-19 virus originated in Wuhan, China, and has since reached all corners of the globe. In March 2020, to help stop the rapid spread of the virus, states issued lockdowns where non-essential employees converted to remote work and students of all

DOI: 10.4324/9781003186076-4

grade levels, including colleges and universities, transitioned to virtual learning. As the virus continued to spread, many states issued mandatory mask mandates and social distancing requirements for all individuals in indoor settings. Personal protective equipment (PPE), such as masks, were in high demand and short supply.

The first COVID-19 vaccines became available to the public in the United States in December 2020. Those 75 years of age and over were given priority. Vaccine campaigns initially targeted nursing homes and assisted living facilities with large elderly populations where cases were high, and populations were most vulnerable. As Americans received the vaccine, there was a decline in the number of cases of COVID-19 and COVID-related deaths. In late spring and early summer, the low number of cases created a sense of a return to normalcy. Mask mandates were lifted and business returned to somewhat normal.

However, in late spring 2021, the Delta variant began spreading in the United States, leading to an increase in cases of COVID-19 and deaths. As the virus continues to spread throughout the United States, the disparate impacts on minority and low-income communities highlight the health inequities that exist in the United States. Phelan et al. (2010) note linkages between social conditions and the causes of health inequities. According to the Centers for Disease Control and Prevention (CDC):

> Health equity is when everyone has the opportunity to be as healthy as possible. Achieving health equity requires valuing everyone equally with focused and ongoing efforts to address avoidable inequities, historical and contemporary injustices, and the elimination of disparities in health and healthcare. The population health impact of COVID-19 has exposed longstanding inequities that have systematically undermined the physical, social, economic, and emotional health of racial and ethnic minority populations and other population groups that are bearing a disproportionate burden of COVID-19.
>
> *CDC, 2021a*

As the virus continues to spread, the National Institute of Environmental Health Sciences, in collaboration with North Carolina State University and Texas A&M developed the Pandemic Vulnerability Index (PVI) (NIEHS, 2021). Through the visualization of population data, scientists, policy makers, and the public can use the data to identify communities most at risk.

The PVI in Figure 3.1 provides data on the location of the most vulnerable communities in the United States. This interactive site provides a PVI score for each city in the United States based on the following criteria:

1) Infection Rate Transmissible Cases, 2) Infection Rate Disease Spread, 3) Population Concentration/Population Mobility, 4) Population Concentration/Residential Density, 5) Intervention/Social Distancing, 6)

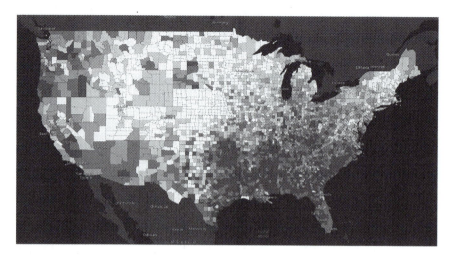

FIGURE 3.1 Vulnerable Communities to COVID-19 in the United States

Intervention/Testing, 7) Health & Environment/Population Demographics, 8) Health & Environment/Air Pollution, 9) Health & Environment/ Age Distribution, 10) Health and Environment/Co-Morbidities, 11) Health & Environment/Health Disparities, and 12) Health and Environment/ Hospital Beds.

NIEHS, 2021

These criteria provide useful indicators of a community's vulnerability to COVID-19. Figure 3.1 shows the locations of the most vulnerable regions in the United States are largely in the southern and midwestern states with some areas in the western and southwest states. This data is publicly available to all and a valuable tool in fighting COVID-19.

When examining the impacts of the pandemic by racial and ethnic groups, those populations with the highest death rate are among American Indians, Alaskan Natives, Blacks, and Hispanics (CDC, 2021b). Black populations had the highest death rate from COVID-19 during the first months of the pandemic, followed by American Indians and Alaskan Natives (AI/AN). However, the death rate for AI/AN was highest among all minority groups during the winter of 2021, followed by Hispanics. The death rate remained highest for AI/AN in summer 2021. Williamson et al. (2021) support these findings that AI and AN have a higher mortality rate than Whites from COVID-19.

When examining the COVID-related deaths by state, data availability and quality of data is an issue. Not all states provide data on COVID cases and COVID-related death broken down by race and ethnicity. California is one state that provides excellent data on COVID and its impacts on minority communities. Latinos are the most highly impacted racial group by COVID-19 in the state in comparison to all other racial/ethnic groups. While Latinos make up 38.9% of the population of California, they account for 53.9% of all COVID-related cases in the State (California Department of Public Health, 2021). Blacks come in second with 5% of the COVID cases while only accounting for 6% of the state's population. By contrast, Asians make up 15.4% of the State's population but only account for 6.8% of COVID cases. Whites make up 36.6% of the population but only account for 21.9% of all COVID cases. As the evidence shows, health inequities exist. This chapter will now explore possible reasons for these health inequities.

Occupational Status and COVID-19

Studies have shown that one of the factors leading to increased risk of exposure to COVID is one's employment (Bailey et al., 2017; Andrasfy and Goldman (2021) 2021; Selden & Berdahl, 2020). While many workers were able to transition to remote work during the pandemic, many others were not afforded that luxury and had to report to work in person. Those reporting to work in person are referred to as "essential workers." Essential workers include white-collar positions with higher occupational standing (OS) where social distancing is observed and frontline workers in high-risk industries including grocery stores, healthcare, sanitation workers, and farm workers.

Goldman et al. (2021) reveal the linkages between OS and COVID-19-related exposures for AI/AN, Blacks, and Hispanics. The authors found while Whites were overrepresented in frontline jobs, AI/AN, Blacks, and Latinos are more likely to hold jobs of lower OS that cannot be done remotely and are therefore at higher risk of exposure to COVID-19 than Whites and Asians. Frontline jobs with lower OS may be less likely to provide proper PPE to mitigate exposure. The authors' findings are consistent with a long history of structural racism and occupational segregation in the United States for a lower occupational status of frontline workers (Bailey et al., 2017).

Bottemiller Erich et al. (2020) found that farm workers faced a disproportionately high rate of infection from COVID-19. When examining rates of COVID-19 infection in California, Washington, Arizona, Oregon, and North Carolina, counties with the highest rates of infection were the top agricultural producers of such products as lettuce, sweet potatoes, and apples. The authors noted the Food and Environment Reporting Network estimated 57,000 food system workers and 6,700 agricultural workers tested positive for COVID-19 as of September 2020.

Murphy, (1998) and Murphy-Greene (2002a, 2002b, 2002c) found farm workers, who are largely Hispanic, were highly at risk of exposure to occupational hazards due to a lack of PPE and basic handwashing facilities and toilets provided by the employers. Current standards by the Occupational Health and Safety Administration do not require basic handwashing facilities or toilets for farm workers working on farms of 11 or fewer workers (OSHA, 2021). The lack of these basic sanitation facilities for farm workers on farms of 11 or fewer workers creates an unsafe and unhealthy working environment. Workers are at high risk of exposure to COVID and other occupational hazards and are more likely to spread the virus due to a lack of access to basic sanitation facilities required for workers in other industries. Farm workers are of lower OS based on a number of factors including the large percentage who are foreigners who do not speak English contributing to their low wages. Additionally, many farm workers are not US citizens and therefore do not have the same social standing as workers in other industries. California and Florida are two of the top agricultural states in the United States. The data on COVID reveals Hispanics in California make up the majority of the COVID cases and deaths. It is time to close the loopholes in the Occupational Health and Safety Standards and requires basic sanitation facilities for the workers who handpick America's fruits and vegetables for minimum pay. The COVID-19 pandemic has shined the light on a long-existing health inequity.

When examining race and occupation, Selden and Berdahl (2020) found employment may be an important pathway to infection for minority workers and household members of those workers. The authors found that 56.6% of high-risk Blacks lived in households with at least one worker who could not work from home, possibly exposing household members to COVID. Additionally, Blacks and Hispanics live in larger households in comparison to Whites. The average size household for Blacks is 3.1 members, 3.8 members for Hispanics, and 2.8 members for Whites. Therefore, Blacks and Hispanics' larger size households could lead to increased exposure among household members. Finally, the authors found that Blacks were more likely to work in frontline positions such as healthcare, public safety, and public utilities, with a higher percentage of Black women in healthcare. Hispanics were more likely to work in frontline food-related jobs. The combination of high-risk frontline jobs and larger household size is most likely a factor in increased exposure and cases of COVID-19 among these minority groups.

COVID-19 Vaccine

In December 2020, the first COVID vaccine became available to the general public for those 18 years of age and older. There are currently three vaccines available in the United States; Pfizer and Moderna requiring two doses and Johnson & Johnson requiring one dose. As previously discussed in this chapter, COVID-related deaths dramatically decreased as more individuals received the vaccine. This data lends support to the effectiveness of the vaccine as the strongest tool for combating the virus. In April 2021, vaccines became available for those 16 years of age and up, and in May 2021, the vaccine was available to those ages 12 and up. This increase in the availability of the vaccine allowed a larger percentage of people in the United States to have access to important protection measures and appears to have made a positive impact on COVID-related cases and deaths in the United States.

TABLE 3.1 Vaccination Rate by State for Fully Vaccinated Individuals as of September 11, 2021

State	Lowest Vaccination Rate (%)	State	Highest Vaccination Rate (%)
West Virginia	39.9	Vermont	68.4
Wyoming	39.9	Conn.	66.9
Idaho	40	Mass.	66.7
Alabama	40	Maine	66.6
Mississippi	40.8	Rhode Island	65.9

Source: Mayo Clinic (2021).

While the vaccine has proven its effectiveness in fighting COVID-19, as of November 1, 2021, only 58.1% of the US population is fully vaccinated and 67.4% of the population has received one dose (Mayo Clinic, 2021). As the more deadly Delta variant continues to spread throughout the United States, many regions of the country still have low vaccination rates as case numbers and deaths have increased. States with the lowest and highest vaccination rates for fully vaccinated individuals are displayed in Table 3.1.

States with the lowest vaccination rates include WV and WY, tied for the lowest with a rate of 39.9% each, followed by ID and AL, with each at 40%, and MS at 40.8%. In contrast, states with the highest vaccination rates are VT with 68.4% fully vaccinated, followed closely by CT, MA, ME, and RI all with just over 66%.

When exploring factors impacting vaccination rates, Hughes et al. (2021) use the CDC's Social Vulnerability Index (SVI) (CDC, 2021c) to interpret vaccination rates in the United States. The SVI consists of five indicators grouped into four themes for a total of 20 metrics. The four themes are: (1) Socioeconomic Status, (2) Household Composition and Disability Status, (3) Racial/Ethnic Minority Status and English, and (4) Household type and Transportation. The authors found that of 49,264,338 people in counties in 49 states and the District of Columbia receiving at least one dose of the vaccine; vaccination rates were higher (15.8%) in counties with low SVI than in high SVI counties (13.9%). The data from these findings was gathered from December 2020 to March 2021; in the first three months, the vaccine was available to the public. Therefore, vaccination rates may appear lower overall. However, it should be noted a nearly 2% difference in vaccination rates is revealed when comparing higher and lower SVI counties. In understanding the impacts on COVID-19 among vulnerable populations, the CDC's SVI is also used to identify at-risk communities (CDC, 2021c). The results highlight the impacts social factors have on vaccination rates in the United States. This chapter will now explore the issue of vaccine hesitancy in the United States and the possible causes behind the low vaccination rates among minority communities in the United States.

COVID-19 Vaccine Hesitancy

Vaccine hesitancy is a major problem in the fight against COVID-19. As previously presented in this chapter, evidence shows Blacks and Hispanics are disproportionately impacted by the virus with a higher morbidity rate than Whites and Asians. Research shows Blacks and Hispanics are more likely to have pre-existing conditions such as diabetes, obesity, and coronary artery disease, which exacerbate the impacts of COVID-19 infection (Kricorian & Turner, 2021; Tai et al., 2021). When examining vaccination rates by racial/ethnic groups in the United States, data reveals lower vaccination rates among AI/AN, Blacks, and Hispanics in comparison to Whites and Asians (CDC, 2021d). Of the total percentage of those fully vaccinated, Blacks and Hispanics represent the lowest percentage overall. This chapter will now explore some of the contributing factors to the low vaccination rates in the Black and Hispanic communities. The information presented will elucidate why African Americans and Hispanics distrust and are hesitant to interact with the medical and public health community in the United States.

When examining the low vaccination rates in Black and Hispanic communities, Kricorian and Turner (2021) reveal several contributing factors. The researchers' findings show Blacks and Hispanics are more hesitant than US Whites to receive the COVID-19 vaccine for the following reasons: (1) They thought the vaccine was dangerous, (2) they could catch COVID-19 from the vaccine, (3) the vaccine was more harmful than getting COVID-19, and (4) they needed more information on the long-term impacts of the vaccine and possible side effects. Additionally, their research shows Blacks and Hispanics were significantly more likely than Whites to indicate they wanted to wait for over a year and were significantly less likely than Whites to indicate that they wanted to get vaccinated immediately or encourage a family member to get vaccinated. The authors also found Blacks were more likely than any other group to feel the COVID vaccine was not something they trusted.

When examining the issue of trust, Kricorian and Turner's (2021) findings reveal several factors within the Black and Hispanic communities contributing to the lack of trust. The researchers found Blacks were more likely than any other group to respond that more testing on people of their own race/ethnicity was needed. They also revealed both Hispanics and Blacks found it very important a medical professional of their own race endorse the vaccine. Both findings indicate a lack of trust with people outside of the Black and Hispanic communities by Blacks and Hispanics. Other studies have shown similar results regarding a lack of trust with medical professionals outside one's racial/ethnic group such as the study by Hernandez et al. (2019) with Latina college women and the HPV vaccine. Historical factors may also be contributing factors for the lack of trust within the Black and Hispanic communities. This chapter will now focus on factors contributing to the lack of trust by Black and Hispanic individuals.

The Legacy of the Tuskegee Study

One major event affecting the lack of trust within the Black community is the US Public Health Service Syphilis Study carried out from 1934 to 1972. The participants in the study were 600 poor Black sharecroppers in Macon County, Alabama, 399 who had syphilis and 201, in the control group, who were told they were given treatment for syphilis, when in fact no treatment was ever administered to any participants (Tuskegee, 2021). The researchers did not obtain informed consent from the participants and many in the study suffered health issues and death from the lack of treatment (Katz et al., 2008). Despite the eventual operational use of penicillin as a cure, the participants were not given treatment (Jones, 1993; Kennedy et al., 2007; Thomas & Quinn, 1991). According to Savitt (1982), African Americans were the objects of experimental medical research and were forced to be "reluctant patients" (p. 105) in the South where they were used for clinical instruction by White medical students and instructors at schools. The reluctance, hesitancy, and fear of public health and the medical community by African Americans are very much justified. If the African American community is distrustful of the medical community, then not only are they subject to avoidance but enrolling them into medical research trials is exceedingly difficult. Therefore, finding treatments and modalities (medicines) suited for their comorbidity and specific healthcare needs that are prevalent in the community is more challenging to address (Opel et al., 2021; Warren et al., 2020).

To illustrate the difficulty of getting African Americans to participate in medical trials, note that the presidents of two of the more prestigious Historically Black Colleges and Universities (Dillard and Xavier) participated in vaccine trials to gather support, but their efforts were thwarted and shunned by the community who viewed this as asking them to allow their children to become experiments for pharmaceutical companies (Moss, 2021). Thus, there exists a situation where a group of people with the highest morbidity and mortality rates from health-related issues will not participate in clinical trials that could greatly help reduce the medical issues in African Americans because of the actions by that very medical community in the past. This is the quintessential "catch-22" (see Joseph Heller, 1961) though all is not lost. The literature reveals that involving African American physicians in the community and other trusted public health professionals of color can build more trust (Warren et al., 2020). Most may agree that tearing or destroying things can be easy but building anything worthwhile takes time and patience. Building trust in the medical and public health community will require significant effort.

In 1997, President Clinton officially apologized for the US government's involvement in this highly unethical medical study and the harm it caused to the hundreds of Black individuals involved in the study and their families (Mitchell, 1997). However, the damage caused by the Tuskegee Study is still felt today in the high level of mistrust toward the US government and the medical community among Blacks in the United States.

In addition to the Tuskegee Study, there were other medical experiments carried out on the African American community (Jaiswala & Halkitis, 2019; Washington, 2008; Xu et al., 2021). It is for these reasons African Americans lack trust. Additionally, combining more recent failures by public health (COVID-19/HIV) and medical communities to address prevalent comorbidities within the African American community, the trust continues to erode (Brancati et al., 2000; Gawlik et al., 2019).

Vaccine Hesitancy and a Lack of Accessibility

Though most of the essential workers in the United States are members of the most socioeconomically disadvantaged, they have also been less likely to have access to much-needed vaccines despite their increased exposure to the COVID-19 virus (Cheng et al., 2020; Nishan, 2020; Phillips et al., 2020; Xu et al., 2021). The initial failure to make vaccines available was due to the federal government's fractured execution of the National Preparedness System (NPS) and Whole Community Approach as noted by the Congressional Research Service (Brown, 2021; CRS, 2021). The disorganized and fractured national response impeded accessibility as well as provided reasons for hesitancy in African American and Hispanic communities. Nonetheless, accessibility and hesitancy (Bunch, 2021) are responsible for the higher rate of deaths among African Americans and Hispanics, which is much greater than those of White Americans (Monnat, 2020; Phillips et al., 2020; Xu et al., 2021). For example, the study by Phillips et al. revealed that though non-Hispanic Blacks (NHBs, African Americans) were only 30% of the population in Chicago, they represented 72% of COVID-19-related deaths, and similar findings were noted in Minnesota, Michigan, and Louisiana et al. (2020). Yet, Whites have received significantly more access and availability to vaccines, ensuring their rate of vaccination far exceeded that of the more underserved and marginalized essential workers (Gardiner, 2020; Mclernon, 2021). The Kaiser Family Foundation (KFF) reported that African Americans and Latinx persons were provided much less vaccine doses in a statistical poll in 23 states and the trend was even greater in at least 20 other states (Mclernon, 2021). Vaccine hesitancy amid mistrust was revealed in at least two polls that posited African Americans trusted their local physicians and healthcare providers (85%) more than Dr. Fauci (77%), the CDC (78%), and trust in former President Trump was 12% (Ndugga et al., 2021). The mistrust in vaccinations can be explained and unfortunately is warranted, given the historically abusive precedents associated with African Americans and the healthcare and medical communities (Bunch, 2021; Jones, 1993; Washington, 2008).

The success of vaccine distribution and inoculation depends largely on public trust (Jamison et al., 2019). For example, a study by Jamison et al. (2019) revealed most Whites trusted the federal government but did not feel the government was competent. A much more poignant question that was not delved into would be why did Whites feel the federal government was incompetent? In contrast, "African Americans were less trusting of the government and were more likely to doubt the motives of federal government institutions. Trust in institutions may be fragile, and once damaged, may take considerable time and effort to repair" (Jamison et al., 2019, p. 1; King, 2003).

There can be no successful defense or debate about the 2020 COVID-19 National Preparedness response that it was not as efficient as it could have been according to the Congressional Research Service (Brown, 2021; CRS, 2021). As noted, part of the failure was poor logistical supply chain distribution of vaccines, production, delivery of diagnostic tests, and insufficient inventory of PPE for essential workers and vulnerable in the American society (CRS, 2021). In January 2021, African American acceptance began to increase partly due to new strategies and ways to reach the communities, such as using the "Health Advocates In-Reach and Research" (HAIR network; McLernon, 2021). An example of this involved the training of barbers to get involved in promoting medical screenings. Churches, barbershops, and other trusted stakeholders in the community will greatly increase trust and ultimately participation of vaccinations within African American communities. For example, the Harris Poll showed an increase from 43% in October 2020 to 58% in January 2021 in African Americans' willingness to get vaccinated (Bulik, 2021). The distrust held by African Americans for the medical and public health community is not solely based on the Tuskegee Study (Bunch, 2021; Jones, 1993) though there is no debate that this historical tragedy created distrust and fear within the African American community regarding public health and the medical profession (Randall, 1996).

Though hesitancy in the African American community has been well documented, there is the question of accessibility to vaccines. There is a disparity in vaccine convenience, which includes availability and access in African American communities. Further, hesitancy in African American communities is due to factors far different than those of Whites (Bunch, 2021). In other words, the behavior being exhibited by the African American community is fueled by *fear* not mere hesitancy for hesitancy's sake and the desire to be vaccinated is much greater than is being projected. Contrarily, there is data that reveals Latinx, and White Americans are more willing to receive COVID-19 vaccinations than African Americans. Gramlich and Funk's (2020) findings revealed 74% of Whites and Latinx were more willing to participate as compared to 54% of African Americans. Bunch's article regarding COVID-19 and hesitancy addressed the question of hesitancy but overlooked a key factor that through such findings, African Americans fear COVID-19 more than Whites (PEW Research Center, 2020); the focus of her research gravitated toward hesitancy as opposed to alternate barriers, such as availability and accessibility. However, her addressing of White's distrust as being related to competency and in contrast African Americans related to the federal institutions' motives as a key factor reveals Whites do not have the horrific lived experiences of medical abuse or victimization from disasters (e.g., hurricanes, flooding, environmental hazards, and so on; Palm & Corbridge, 1983; Pulido, 2008; Wilson, 2020) that is ingrained and embedded in the socio-psyche of African Americans in the United States (Adams et al., 2006).

The probability that African Americans' desire vaccination despite their mistrust of the public health and medical system was documented in the March 2021 survey by the National Public Radio/Public Broadcasting Station NewsHour Marist Poll. The study noted 73% of African Americans and 70% of White Americans planned to get vaccinated at that time (Summers, 2021). Perhaps the hesitancy within the African American community is not as salient as thought. Data regarding the matter of access posits that when provided with the opportunity to receive vaccinations, African Americans are more than willing. This fact was observed when federally funded vaccination programs for children were made available to the African American communities and the rate of vaccinations was not significantly different than that of Whites (Walker et al., 2014). The real issue is a lack of medical practitioners and facilities in African American communities, thus restricting access to preventive health. The location of African American communities makes the prospect of opening businesses or medical practices less appetizing. Redlining and urban planning contributed to today's racially segregated communities (Palm & Corbridge, 1982; Wilson, 2020). Communities of color are often located near railroad tracks, industrial and manufacturing plants, and in precariously exposed landscapes ripe for natural disasters. Historic redlining practices and urban planning has contributed to the segregation and furtherance of socio-economic and healthcare disparities in the United States (Roberts & Rizzo, 2021). This has meant many communities of color do not have financial institutions, grocery stores, or medical healthcare facilities within them, so all that ails and threatens these communities continue to grow and metastasize like a social cancer.

Building Trust in Minority Communities: Strategies for Resiliency

African American and Hispanic communities are heavily influenced by community social interactions fostered by houses of worship, doctors of color within the community (African American, Latinx), and businesses, such as barbershops and nail salons, and so on, which can enhance trust and increase participation in vaccination inoculations (McLernon, 2021). According to Dr. De Veranez (personal communication, September 2021), a practicing African American physician in Atlanta, Georgia, she anecdotally agreed that her experience with her African American patients is that the majority have been willing to get vaccinated when provided access or by seeing a picture of her getting vaccinated in her exam rooms. Despite African Americans' traumatic and sordid relationship with the United States' public health and medical communities (King, 2003; Thomas &

Quinn, 1991; Washington, 2008), particularly those in the South, the belief that the community is singularly hesitant may be misleading. Present beliefs and optics about whether the African American community are amicable to vaccinations needs more investigation within specified contextual situations, given the findings by the CDC morbidity and mortality weekly report (Walker et al., 2014). Merely accepting or buying into the premise that the African American and Hispanic communities are resistant and hesitant is too convenient for letting the public health and medical community get away with not making healthcare to this group more accessible.

Whole Community Approach Means All of the United States

The impact of focusing events from onset hazards (natural, technological, and human-made disaster) are often so large in scale, intensity, and scope that the coping capacity and resources of a jurisdiction (local, county, state, territory, tribe) are exceeded (Brown, 2018). A way to make up for jurisdictions and communities' lack of resources is to combine and collaborate resources with others, for example, emergency management assistance compacts (EMAC, 2021), which was,

> ratified by U.S. Congress (PL 104–321) and is law in all 50 states, the District of Columbia, Puerto Rico, Guam, the U.S. Virgin Islands and the Northern Mariana Islands, and allows for shared resources to ensure increased capabilities to prepare for, and respond to disasters.
>
> *p. 1*

Of course, the EMACs were overtasked and not able to provide the mutual aid, given the size, scope, and intensity of the COVID-19 pandemic. Nevertheless, the Whole Community Approach (FEMA, 2011) is an effort by the federal government to exercise inclusiveness and to have all the American society provide their resources toward national preparedness. It is an integral part of the NPS and a way for the country to achieve the National Preparedness Goal (NPG). The approach involves reaching out to and having the whole American community get involved in the building of a more resilient and sustainable preparedness system. Included are: (1) All individuals and families, (2) private businesses, (3) faith-based and non-governmental organizations, (4) medical/health-care and educational institutions, (5) media and social media platforms, and (6) federal, state, local, territories, and tribes gathered to help prepare the United States for challenges to safety and security and build a more resilient and sustainable community (Brown, 2021; FEMA, 2011).

The Whole Community Approach sounds noble, and from a practical standpoint, such a concept can provide the much-needed resources necessary to better prepare the nation for challenges to its safety and security, and to prepare underserved and marginalized communities to overcome their reality of dearth resources.

If the cliché hindsight is 2020 has any merit hopefully the events of fiscal year 2020 revealed that not all American citizens were included in the Whole Community approach, thus leaving a hole in ensuring a successful national response to the Coronavirus SARS-CoV-2 (COVID-19) pandemic (Brown, 2021; CRS, 2021). African Americans make up the largest portion of essential workers in the United States and African American women are a large part of this vulnerable group. In this country, African American women disproportionately experience oppressive living standards and increased risk. For example, they are four times likely to die giving childbirth, and die at twice the rate of White females from hypertensive cardiovascular disease (Sherwin, 1992). Yet, they lag in wages, make up a large majority of those persons, who are cashiers, food servers, and take care of our elderly. It appears that important parts of the "Whole Community" have yet to be achieved.

Health Equity Strategy: Building Resilient Communities

In order to address some of the shortfalls of the current approach to fighting the COVID-19 virus, the CDC is currently implementing the new Health Equity Strategy (HES). The HES incorporates several of the strategies used in the Whole Community Approach, with a few additions. The five main principles of this strategy include:

- Expand the evidence base.
- Use data-driven approaches.
- Foster meaningful engagement with community institutions and diverse leaders.
- Lead culturally responsive outreach.
- Reduce stigma, including stigma associated with race and ethnicity (CDC, 2021e).

The HES builds on the Whole Community Approach involving community institutions and diverse leaders while focusing on culturally responsive outreach. Yet it also includes data-driven approaches to help focus resources where they are most needed within vulnerable communities. This new strategy allows public health officials and policy makers to use the best available data to drive target community outreach efforts and help address long-existing health inequities throughout the United States.

Conclusion

This chapter provides insight into the issue of health equity as it pertains to the current battle against COVID-19. While the pandemic has taken the lives of hundreds of thousands of Americans and millions worldwide, much progress has been made since the pandemic was first declared. The virus has shined the light on long-standing health inequities that have existed throughout the United States for decades. Addressing existing health inequities will also involve addressing the lack of trust that exists today with the African American and Latino populations and the medical community. As a result, more resources and research are now focusing on addressing the public health of all communities in the United States, especially the most vulnerable.

While school-aged children and university students headed back to in-person classes in fall 2021 for the first time since the pandemic began, many businesses and government offices have reinstated mask mandates. However, with increased expansion of vaccinations for all those eligible in the United States, using the Whole Community Approach and the HES, communities throughout the United States will strengthen their resiliency using the best available data and knowledge to fight the COVID-19 virus and any future public health crisis.

Review/Discussion Questions

1. How do you think the Tuskegee Study impacted vaccination efforts in the fight against COVID-19 in the United States?
2. What are some ways to help build trust in minority communities with medical professionals?
3. What actions by state and local politicians do you think could be done to help develop a more equal and just social infrastructure within marginalized communities?
4. How can the federal, state, and local governments as well as private industries build trust within the African American community with regard to research and medical/ public health treatment?

References

Adams, G., O'Brien, L. T., & Nelson, J. C. (2006). Perceptions of racism in hurricane Katrina: A liberation psychology analysis. *Analyses of Social Issues and Public Policy, 6*(1), 215–235.

Andrasfy T. and Goldman, N. (2021). Reductions in 2020 US life expectancy due to COVID-19 and the disproportionate impact on the Black and Latino population. *Proceedings of the National Academy of Sciences, 118*(5), 1–15.

Bailey, Z. D., Krieger, N., Age´nor, M., Graves, J., Linos, N., Bassett, M. T. (2017). Structural racism and health inequities in the USA: Evidence and interventions. *The Lancet, 389*, 1453–1463.

Brancati, B., Kao, F. L., Folsom, W. H., Watson, A. R., & Szklo, R. L. (2000). Incident type 2 diabetes mellitus in African American and White adults: The atherosclerosis risk in communities study. *Journal of American Medical Association, 283*, 2253–2259.

Brown, M. A. (2018). Building resilient communities before and after the hurricanes. In *William Lester, Transforming Disaster Response: Federalism and Leadership* (pp. 112–147). Routledge, New York, NY.

Brown, M. A. (2021). National preparedness failure: Hindsight is 2020. Retrieved on September 8, 2021 from https://domprep.com/preparedness/national-preparedness-failure-hindsight-is-2020/Bulik, B. S. (2021). Good news for shot-makers: COVID-19 vaccine leaps to 69%, Harris poll finds. Retrieved on September 20, 2021 from www.fiercepharma.com/marketing/covid-19-vaccine-confidence-ticks-up-intent-to-get-a-vaccine-near-pandemic-start-harris.

Bunch, L. (2021). A tale of two crises: Addressing COVID-19 vaccine hesitancy as promoting racial justice. Retrieved on September 8, 2021 from https://doi.org/10.1007/s10730-021-09440-0.

California Department of Public Health. (2021). COVID-19 race and ethnicity data. Retrieved on September 8, 2021 from www.cdph.ca.gov/Programs/CID/DCDC/Pages/COVID-19/Race-Ethnicity.aspx#

Center for Disease Control and Prevention. (2021a). Health Equity Considerations for Racial and Ethnic Minority Groups. COVID Retrieved on February 15, 2021 from from https://covid.cdc.gov/covid-data-tracker/#trends_dailycases.

Center for Disease Control and Prevention. (2021b). COVID-19 weekly cases and deaths per 100,000 population by race/ethnicity. Retrieved on September 10, 2021 from https://covid.cdc.gov/covid-data-tracker/#demographicsovertime.

Center for Disease Control and Prevention. (2021c). COVID 19 vaccine equity. Retrieved on September 10, 2021 from https://covid.cdc.gov/covid-data-tracker/#vaccination-equity.

Center for Disease Control and Prevention. (2021d). COVID tracker data: Percent of people receiving COVID-19 vaccine by race/ethnicity. Retrieved on September 13, 2021 from https://covid.cdc.gov/covid-data-tracker/#demographicsovertime.

Center for Disease Control and Prevention. (2021e). Health equity data. Retrieved on September 10, 2021 from https://covid.cdc.gov/covid-data-tracker/#health-equity-data.

Cheng, K. J. G., Sun, Y., & Monnat, S. M. (2020). COVID-19 death rates are higher in rural counties with larger shares of Blacks and Hispanics. *Journal Rural Health*, *36*(4), 602–608.

Congressional Research Service (CRS). (2021). National preparedness: A summary and select issues. Retrieved on September 10, 2021 from https://fas.org/sgp/crs/homesec/R46696.pdf.

Emergency Management Assistance Compact (EMAC). (2021). The all hazards national mutual aid system. Retrieved on September 9, 2021 from https://emacweb.org/

Erich, B., et al. (2020, September 8). Harvest of shame: Farmworkers face coronavirus disaster. *Politico*. Retrieved on September 20, 2021 from www.politico.com/news/2020/09/08/farmworkers-coronavirus-disaster-409339.

Federal Emergency Management Agency (FEMA). (2011). A whole community approach to emergency management: Principles, themes, and pathways for action. Retrieved on September 8, 2021 from www.fema.gov/sites/default/files/2020-07/whole_community_dec2011__2.pdf.

Gardiner, B. (2020). *Unequal Impact: The Deep Links between Racism and Climate Change.* Yale School of the Environment, New Haven, CT. Retrieved from https://e360.yale.edu/features/unequal-impact-the-deep-links-between-inequality-and-climate-change

Gawlik, K. S., Menyk, B. M., & Tan, A. (2019). Associations between stress and cardiovascular disease risk factors among million hearts priority populations. Retrieved on September 10, 2021 from https://pubmed.ncbi.nlm.nih.gov/31079467.

Goldman, N., Pebley, A., Lee, K, Andrasfay, T., Pratt, B. (2021). Racial and ethnic differencials in COVID-19-related job exposures by occupational standing in the U.S. *PLoS ONE*, *16*(9), 1–17.

Gramlich, J., & Funk, G. (2020). Black Americans face higher COVID-19 risks, are more hesitant to trust medical scientists, get vaccinated. Pew Research Center. Retrieved on September 9, 2021 from https://link.springer.com/article/10.1007/s10 730-021-09440-0.

Hernandez, N., Daley, E., Young, L., Kolar, S., Wheldon, C., Vamos, C., et al. (2019). HPV vaccine recommendation: Does a health care provider's gender and ethnicity matter to Unvaccinated Latina College Women? *Ethnicity and Health*, *24*(6), 645–661.

Hughes, M., et al. (2021). County-level COVID-19 vaccination coverage and social vulnerability-United States, December 14, 2020-March, 1, 2021. Morbidity and Mortality Weekly, *70*(12), 431–436.

Jaiswal, J., & Halkitis, P. N. (2019). Towards a more inclusive and dynamic understanding of medical mistrust informed by science. *Behavioral Medicine*, *45*(2): 79–85. doi:10.1080/08964289.2019.1619511.

Jamison, A. M., Quinn, S. C., & Freimuth, V. S. (2019, January). "You don't trust a government vaccine": Narratives of institutional trust and influenza vaccination among African American and white adults. *Social Science Medicine*, *221*, 87–94. doi:10.1016/j.socscimed.2018.12.020.

Johns Hopkins University. (2021). Center for Systems Science and Engineering (CSSE). Retrieved on November 3, 2021 from www.arcgis.com/apps/dashboards/bda759474 0fd40299423467b48e9ecf6.

Joseph Heller (1961). Catch 22. Retrieved from www.merriam-webster.com/dictionary/catch-22

Jones, J. H. (1993). *Bad Blood: The Tuskegee Syphilis Experiment*. Free Press, New York, NY.

Katz, R., et al. (2008). Awareness of the Tuskegee Syphilis Study and the US presidential apology and their influence on minority participation in biomedical research. Research and Practice, *98*(6), 1137–1142.

Kennedy, B. R., Mathis, C. C., & Woods, A. K. (2007, Summer). African American and their distrust of the health care system: Healthcare for the diverse populations. *Journal of Cultural Diversity*, *14*(2), 56–60.

King, W. D. (2003). Examining African American' mistrust of the health care system: Expanding the research question. *Public Health Reports*, *118*, 366–367.

Kricorian, K., & Turner, K. (2021). COVID-19 vaccine acceptance and beliefs among Black and Hispanic Americans. *PLoS One*, *16*(8), 1–14.

Mayo Clinic. (2021). Mayo Clinic U.S. COVID vaccine tracker. Retrieved on September 11, 2021 from www.mayoclinic.org/coronavirus-covid-19/vaccine-tracker.

McLernon, L. M. (2021). Experts seek to allay COVID vaccine hesitancy in Black Americans. Centers for Infectious Disease Research and Policy. Retrieved on September 9, 2021 from www.cidrap.umn.edu/news-perspective/2021/02/experts-seek-allay-covid-vaccine-hesitancy-black-americans.

Meerow, S., Pajaouhesh, P., & Miller, T. (2019) Social Equity in Urban Resilience Planning. *Local Environment*, *24*(9), 793–808.

Mitchell, A. (1997). Clinton Regrets 'Clearly Racist' U.S. Study. *New York Times*. Sect. 1. p. 10.

Monnat, S. (2020). Mortality rate higher for US rural residents. Retrieved on September 9, 2021 from https://medicalxpress.com/news/2020-10-mortality-higher-rural-reside nts.html.

Moss, L. (2021). Clinical trials have a tarnished reputation in minority communities, but the pharmaceutical industry can fix that. Retrieved on September 29, 2021 from https://hbcuconnect.com/content/362541/clinical-trials-have-a-tarnished-reputation-in-minority-communities-but-the-pharmaceutical-industry-can-fix-that.

Murphy, C. (1998). A theoretical view of environmental justice: Achieving equal protection? *Journal of Public Management and Social Policy, 4*(2), 165–180.

Murphy-Greene, C., & Leip, L. (2002a). Assessing the effectiveness of executive order 12898: Environmental justice for all? *Public Administration Review, 62*(6), 650–658.

Murphy-Greene, C., & Leip, L. (2002b). The occupational safety and health of Florida farm workers: Environmental injustice in the fields? *Journal of Health and Human Services Administration, 25*(3), 281–314.

Murphy, C., and Leip, L. (2002c). "Environmental justice: A case study of farm workers in South Florida. *International Journal of Public Administration, 25*(2/3), 193–220.

National Institute of Environmental Health Sciences. (2021). COVID-19 pandemic vulnerability index. Retrieved on September 8, 2021 from https://covid19pvi.niehs.nih.gov/.

Ndugga, N., Pham, O., Hill, L., Artiga, S., Alam, R., & Parker, N. (2021). Latest data on COVID-19 vaccination race/ethnicity. Retrieved from www.kff.org/coronavirus-covid-19/issue-brief/latest-data-on-covid-19-vaccinations-race-ethnicity/

Nishan, D. (2020, June). Ten ways that racial and environmental justice are inextricably linked. Forbes. Retrieved from www.forbes.com/sites/nishandegnarain/2020/06/30/eight-ways-that-the-fight-for-racial-and-environmental-justice-are-inextricably-linked/?sh=d18549b87321

Occupational Safety and Health Administration. (2021). Occupational Safety and Health Standards for Agriculture. Retrieved on September 24, 2021 from www.osha.gov/laws-regs/regulations/standardnumber/1928/1928.110.

Opel, D. J., Lo, B., & Peek, M. E. (2021, May). Addressing mistrust about COVID-19 vaccines among patients of color. *Annals of Internal Medicine.* Retrieved on September 9, 2021 from www.acpjournals.org/doi/full/10.7326/M21-0055?journalCode=aim.

Palm, R., & Corbridge, J. (1983). The unintended impacts of anti-redlining legislation. *Journal of Environmental Systems, 12*(4), 341–350.

Pew Research Center. (2020). Health concerns from Covid-19 much higher among Hispanics and Blacks than Whites. Retrieved on September 9, 2021 from www.pewresearch.org/politics/2020/04/14/health-concerns-from-covid-19-much-higher-among-hispanics-and-blacks-than-whites/

Phelan, J. C., Link, B. G., & Tehranifar, P. (2010). Social conditions as fundamental causes of health inequalities: Theory, evidence, and policy implications. *Journal of Health and Social Behavior, 51*, S28–S40.

Phillips, N., Park, I., Robinson, J. R., & Jones, H. P. (2020). The perfect storm: COVID-19 health disparities in US Blacks. *Journal of Racial and Ethnic Health Disparities.* Retrieved from https://doi.org/10.1007/s40615-020-00871-y.

Pulido, L. (2008). Rethinking environmental racism: White privilege and urban development in Southern California. In Ed. Anderson, K. and Braun. B. *Environment: Critical Essays in Human Geography* (pp. 532–577). London: Routledge.

Randall, V. R. (1995). Slavery, segregation and racism: Trusting the health care system ain't always easy: An African American perspective on bioethics. Retrieved on September 9, 2021 from https://academic.udayton.edu/health/05bioethics/slavery03.htm.

Randall, V. R. (1996). Distrust and bioethical issues. Retrieved on September 29, 2021 from https://academic.udayton.edu/health/05bioethics/slavery03.htm.

Roberts, S. O., & Rizzo, M. T. (2021). The psychology of American Racism. *American Psychologist, 76*(3), 475–487.

Savitt, T. L. (1982). The use of blacks for medical experimentation and demonstration in the Old South. *The Journal of Southern History, 48*(3), 331–348.

Selden, T. M., & Berdahl, T. A. (2020). COVID-19 and racial/ethnic disparities in health risk, employment, and household composition. *Health Affairs, 39*(9), 1624–1632.

Sheahan, T., & Frieman, M. (2020). The continued epidemic threat of SARS-CoV2 and implications for the future of global public health. Current Opinion in Virology, *40*, 37–40.

Sherwin, S. (1992). *No Longer Patient: Feminist Ethics and Healthcare.* Temple University Press, New York, NY.

Summers, J. (2021, March). Little difference in vaccine hesitancy among White and Black Americans, poll finds. Retrieved from www.npr.org/sections/coronavirus-live-updates/2021/03/12/976172586/little-difference-in-vaccine-hesitancy-among-white-and-black-americans-poll-find.

Tai, D. B. G., Shah, A., Doubeni, C. A., Sia, I. G., & Wieland, M. L. (2021). The disproportionate impact of COVID-19 on racial and ethnic minorities in the United States. Clinical Infectious Disease, *72*(4), 703–770.

Thomas, S. B., & Quinn, S. C. (1991). The Tuskegee syphilis study, 1932 to 1972: Implications for HIV education and AIDS risk education programs in the Black community. *American Journal of Public Health, 81*(11), 1498–1505.

Tuskegee University. (2021). About the USPHS syphilis study. Accessed on September 23, 2021 www.tuskegee.edu/about-us/centers-of-excellence/bioethics-center/about-the-usphs-syphilis-study.

Walker, A. T., Smith, P. J., & Kolasa, M. (2014). Reduction of racial/ethnic disparities in vaccination coverage, 1995–2011. *Morbidity and Mortality Report, 63*(01), 7–12.

Warren, R. C., Farrow, L., Hodge, D. A., & Truog, R. D. (2020). Trustworthiness before trust: Covid-19 vaccine trials and the black community. Retrieved from www.nejm.org/doi/full/10.1056/NEJMp2030033

Washington, H. A. (2008). *Medical Apartheid: The Dark History of Medical Experimentation on Black Americans from Colonial Times to the Present.* Anchor Books, New York, NY.

Williamson, E. J. et al. (2021). COVID-19 incidence and mortality among American Indian/Alaskan native and white persons-Montana, March 13-November, 30, 2020. Morbidity and mortality weekly report. U.S. Health and Human Services/Center for Disease Control and Prevention. April 9, 2021 *70*(14), 510–513.

Wilson, B. (2020). Urban heat management and the legacy of redlining. *Journal of the American Planning Association, 86*(4), 443–457. doi:10.1080/01944363.2020.1759127.

World Health Organization. (2021). Timeline: WHO's COVID-19 response. Retrieved on September 8, 2021 from www.who.int/emergencies/diseases/novel-coronavirus-2019/interactive-timeline?gclid=CjwKCAjwvuGJBhB1EiwACU1AidKXA10NS8-9RGQvJTq20BhsaBEQGlogEQV3Ejlcy_y2RGpB84cF0RoCWBYQAvD_BwE#!

Xu, J. J., Chen, J. T., Belin, T. R., Brookmeyer, R. S., Suchard, M. A., & Ramirez, C. M. (2021). Racial and ethnic disparities in years of potential life lost attributable to COVID-19 in the United States: An analysis of 45 states and the District of Columbia. *Environmental Research and Public Health, 18*, 1–29. https://doi.org/10.3390/ijerph18062921.

4

THE FLINT WATER CRISIS

Chris R. Surfus and Cara Sanner

Introduction

On April 24, 2014, the City of Flint, Michigan, began to draw its water from the Flint River. This set off a chain of events that would become one of the greatest US public health crises to result from lead contamination of a community water supply. The colossal failure of Flint citizens by government officials that became the Flint Water Crisis has roots in an earlier state action. This chapter will cover the steps leading up to the Flint Water Crisis, the impact of the decision made by state government officials on the Flint community, lessons learned, and ways to increase community resiliency.

On November 7, 2011, the State of Michigan declared a financial emergency in the City of Flint (State of Michigan, 2011). The declaration gave the State the authority to appoint an outside entity as a temporary emergency manager (EM) to handle city operations, thus limiting community access and influence in policy- and decision-making. Krings et al. (2018) discuss the role of EMs and state that

> Michigan has been one of 16 US states with a provision for the state government to shift local decision-making authority away from elected city leaders to an appointed EM under conditions of financial distress (Scorsone, 2014). The EM—whose job is to balance the city's budget without raising taxes or renegotiating debt with creditors—is accountable to the governor and State Treasury Department officials rather than to city council members, thereby reducing opportunities for citizen groups to influence local policies (Lee et al., 2016).
>
> *Krings et al., 2018, p. 585*

DOI: 10.4324/9781003186076-5

This action by the State of Michigan circumvented the role of a democratically elected city council.

A Deadly Decision

To present a balanced budget, Flint's EM began to explore ways to save money by changing the City's water source. For the past nearly 50 years, Flint received its water from Detroit through an agreement with the Great Lakes Water Authority (formerly the regional Detroit Water and Sewerage Department). A proposal was made to reduce costs by joining the new regional Karegnondi Water Authority (Krings et al., 2018, p. 586). The projected cost savings were $200 million over 25 years; an amount great enough to convince officials to move forward with the proposal and join the Karegnondi Water Authority. The following day, Detroit officials announced the termination of water services to the City of Flint, to be effective a year later (NPR, 2016). It is this need for an interim water supply that led to the fateful decision to draw water from the Flint River.

Krings et al. (2018) describe how the shift to decision-making at the state level resulted in an action that would have been quickly rebuked had it come from local leaders:

> Pressure on the EM to cut costs coupled with the impending end of the Detroit contract led to hasty decisions, with minimal regulatory oversight or citizen input. Because of the EM, this decision did not require a vote by city council and likely would not have received public support given the widespread perception that the river was contaminated by decades of industrial waste (Longley, 2011).
>
> *Krings et al., 2018, p. 585*

Flint had been obtaining water from Detroit since 1967 that did not require any further treatment. The Flint Water Treatment Plant (WTP) was built in 1954 but was only used as an emergency backup system to process water from the Flint River if needed. The plant did not receive adequate or regular testing to ensure if it was still capable of effectively treating water. It needed substantial repairs (Hammer, 2019, p. 111). Yet, as a cost-saving measure, rather than continuing to source water from Detroit, which was an option but at a higher rate, the EM determined that the WTP would be capable of processing water from the Flint River for the interim period until water could be supplied by the Karegnondi Water Authority. Krings et al. (2018) discuss some of the fiscal constraints by stating that,

> Due to cost and time constraints, upgrades needed for the water plant were severely underfunded: four months before the switch, the city spent just $3.8 million (Adams, 2014b), even though a 2011 Rowe Engineering report estimated that around $60 million in upgrades were required to make the

river treatment plant a safe, full-time source of drinking water (Longley, 2011). Despite these difficulties, on April 25, 2015, city and state officials raised glasses of water to celebrate as water began to flow from the Flint River.

Krings et al., 2018, p. 586

As water from the Flint River began supplying residential homes, state and local officials knew that there was a risk that the highly corrosive nature of the Flint River was likely to cause leaching from lead-based piping and soldering used to deliver water. A report, commissioned by Flint in 2011, indicated that phosphate would be required to make the river water safe to drink. Phosphate is used to control corrosion by creating a scale layer in pipes and forming a barrier against the corrosive water. The report estimated the cost to treat the water to prevent leaching of lead from pipes to be $60 per day (Kaffer, 2015). However, officials opted to adopt a wait-and-see approach and did not perform the treatment to stop lead corrosion. When confronted with the lack of corrosion control, Michigan Department of Environmental Quality (MDEQ) spokesman Brad Wurfel suggested that the city needed time to understand the correct treatment. Smith (2015) stated that

It's just a matter of getting it right. You know if I handed you a bag of chocolate chips and sack of flour and said, 'make chocolate chips cookies,' we'd still need a recipe, right? And they need to get the results from that testing to understand how much of what to put in the water to address the water chemistry from the river which is different from the water chemistry in Lake Huron.

p. 13

Water sourced from Detroit was historically treated to control corrosion. Yet when presented with clear opportunities to safeguard the health and well-being of Flint residents by treating water drawn from the Flint River, state representatives instead offered patronizing excuses for their inaction.

Under Environmental Protection Agency (EPA)'s Lead and Copper Rule (LCR), localities are required to monitor drinking water for customer taps. If certain levels are exceeded, steps must be taken to control corrosion and the public must be notified (Environmental Protection Agency, 2007, 2019). However, since the LCR monitoring pool in Flint did not have 50% homes with lead service lines as required, and other sampling methods known to reduce the detection of lead in water were used, officials claimed that the city was compliant with the LCR through 2014 and 2015 (Pieper, Tang, & Edwards, 2017).

The MDEQ is charged with enforcing EPA standards and agreed to this approach to the City's compliance with LCR requirements. This decision, according to Dana and Tuerkheimer (2017), was deeply criticized in the Governor's Water Task

Force report, which made clear "that the time it began drawing water from the highly corrosive Flint River [April 24, 2014], MDEQ officials were under a legal obligation to implement corrosion control measures (State of Michigan, 2016, p. 9)" (p. 881). In September 2015, 16 months after the city made the switch in the water supply, an analysis of Flint River water against Detroit water found that the Flint River water leaches 19 times more lead from plumbing than Detroit water (Siddhartha, 2015).

Consequences of Deadly Decision

Using the legal system to create counteracting authority for EMs over democratically elected local governments has led to a breach of public trust. Krings et al. (2018) identify the breach of the public trust by stating that

> The consequences of the swift undemocratic process by which the city switched to the Flint River water were almost immediately apparent: residents complained that their water was discolored, bad tasting, and foul smelling. As the water quality worsened, residents had few outlets to report their problems because the city council had limited authority and the Office of the Ombudsman had been eliminated. When complaints about the water quality were made, representatives of the agencies charged with monitoring the safety of the water—the MDEQ and the Flint Department of Public Works—sought to reassure the public.
>
> *Krings et al., 2018, p. 586*

Residents were experiencing significant impacts as demonstrated by testimony given by Nakiya Wakes on March 23, 2017, at the Trinity Wall conference, Water Justice. Wakes moved with her family to Flint in 2013. Between April and August of 2015, Wakes experienced the pregnancy loss of twins over two separate occasions. Only after the loss of her second pregnancy did she receive notification from the City of Flint stating that pregnant women and people aging 55 and older should not be drinking the City's tap water. Wakes had her children tested and their lead levels were 5.0 [micrograms per deciliter (μg/dL)], which is the Centers for Disease Control and Prevention (CDC) blood lead reference value for children with elevated lead levels. She reported that her daughter's hair was falling out and everyone in the family developed rashes. Wake's son developed behavioral problems (Centers for Disease Control and Prevention, 2021a; Wakes, 2018, pp. 143–144). The CDC uses the blood level reference value of 5 μg/dL to identify children with blood lead levels that are much higher than most children ages one to five, representing the top 2.5% of children tested (Centers for Disease Control and Prevention, 2021b).

As Spring 2015 gave way to summer, and summer to fall and fall to winter, one red flag after another was raised, which should have given state and local officials pause to reconsider their decision to draw water from the Flint River. In August, there were findings of *Escherichia coli* bacteria in the water, and in September, coliform bacteria. Residents were advised to boil their water. There was an outbreak of Legionnaires' disease, which is caused by bacteria and can often lead to pneumonia. Multiple deaths were reported but it was not attributed to the water at that time. In December, General Motors switched its water hookup to neighboring Flint Township. They cited high chloride levels in the water to its engine plant, but there were also reports that the Flint River water was causing parts to rust (Dixon, 2019). In January 2015, total trihalomethanes (TTHMs), a disinfectant byproduct that can cause liver and kidney problems with long-term exposure, had exceeded federal limits. That same month, the University of Michigan began testing its water and detected lead in drinking fountains. A scientists' meeting at City Hall was held and concerned residents showed up to protest the lack of action by authorities, bringing with them jugs of discolored water (Dixon, 2019).

Krings et al. (2018) discuss how despite the clear evidence of health impacts to Flint residents, and the call for action by community leaders, it took even further intervention to secure action by state officials:

> Citizen complaints alone were not sufficiently able to convince city officials or national media of widespread illness caused by the water. However, their efforts resulted in partnerships with researchers whose evidence bolstered their claims, thus inspiring a large contribution from a local foundation to support the switch to a clean water source. Thus, before the crisis gained national media attention, and despite significant constraints, residents' sustained organization—coupled with scientific evidence that credentialed local claims—motivated the return to the Detroit water system.
>
> *p. 583*

Several individuals were instrumental in the reversal of the City's decision to use Flint River water. Dr. Mona Hanna-Attisha was responsible for compiling data establishing the increase in blood lead levels in children in Flint. The director of the Hurley Medical Center Pediatric Residency Program, Hanna-Attisha, first began gathering data on the Hurley Children's Clinic patients. Hanna-Attisha immediately identified an increase in elevated blood lead levels in children compared to before the city switched its water source. She then accessed all available data for children in Flint and discovered that the number of kids with elevated blood levels had nearly doubled in the time that the City began sourcing water from the Flint River. After consultation with area doctors, a press conference was held to reveal findings. It was this group of physicians that called on the City to reverse course and change the water supply back to Lake Huron supplied water from the Great Lakes Water Authority (Smith, 2015).

The severity of the issue was finally brought to the attention of the EPA when Flint resident LeeAnne Walters had her home tested in February 2015 (Dixon,

2019). According to Lotto Persio (2018, p. 5), "While state authorities insisted the water was safe, Walters enlisted the help of the Environmental Protection Agency's (EPA) 'rogue' regional manager Miguel Del Toral and Virginia Tech professor Marc Edwards to make her case while gathering evidence." In August 2015, Edwards notified the MDEQ that he would begin a study of Flint's water quality. Edwards had concerns about corrosion and lead at the outset. He had spent the last ten years lobbying EPA's Office of Ground Water and Drinking Water to recognize the seriousness of the concerns about lead in water (Dixon, 2019). Walters, working under the direction of Edwards, sampled each zip code in Flint, collecting over 800 water samples (Lotto Persio, 2018). It is in large part this effort that ensured state and local officials could no longer ignore the poisoning of Flint residents. On October 16, 2015, the communities' water supply was switched back to Lake Huron water.

The corrosivity and poor environmental quality of the Flint River can be traced to many sources: Biological waste, treated and untreated human and industrial wastes, and contaminants washed into the river by the elements. However, it is primarily the dumping of industrial wastes that can account for much of the pollution of the water. Decades of industrial waste dumping is a sad legacy of the Flint River. This started as early as the 1830s with lumber mills situated on the river, followed by paper mills and chemical processing. The automobile industry followed. Oral accounts going as far back as the 1930s document pollution concerns. In 1960, the Michigan Water Resources Commission gave Flint three years to address point source polluters. This included factories and paper and packaging companies. In 1967, Flint first switched from the Flint River to Lake Huron water processed by Detroit over water quality and shortage concerns. There were many points and non-point sources of pollution: Heavy fertilizer use in rural areas upstream, legacy dumps and landfills, road salt on the city's bridges, General Motors non-compliance with EPA regulations for much of the 1980s, rampant illegal industrial waste dumping activities, sewage spills as a result of combined storm and sewer drains, and the City continued discharge of untreated sewage into the river well into the 2000s (Carmody, 2016; Stein, 1972).

The United Way of Genesee County, Michigan, estimated in 2016 that between 6,000 and 12,000 children were exposed to elevated levels of lead in water during the Flint Water Crisis. According to Landrigan and Bellinger (2016), they state that

> Lead damages children's brains, erodes intelligence, diminishes creativity and the ability to weigh consequences and make good decisions, impairs language skills, shortens attention span, and predisposes to hyperactive and aggressive behavior. Lead exposure in early childhood is linked to later increased risk for dyslexia and school failure. When lead exposure is widespread, it can undermine the economic productivity and sustainability of entire societies.

Factors related to the built environment added to the lead exposure impacts. Sadler et al. (2017) state that

> In Flint, the widespread water-based lead contamination was exacerbated in neighborhoods where water was resident in the pipes for the longest period of time and compounded in neighborhoods known to have higher lead risks, including older homes in poor condition. These factors synergistically increased children's lead exposure.
>
> *p. 768*

Demographics of Flint

It's difficult to imagine the circumstances and chain of events unfolding in the same manner had Flint been a predominantly Caucasian populace or had residents been of a higher socioeconomic class. The US Census Bureau estimates the Flint population at 102,230 residents in 2010, which comprises 54% African American, 4% Hispanic, and 5% other minority ethnicities. From 2013 to 2017, the projected median household income was $26,330, with a per capita income of $15,622 and a median home value of $28,200. Forty-one percent of the population is experiencing poverty (US Census, 2018, 2019). Residents were challenged to influence policy because they lacked access and resources. Martinez (2016) writes that

> Because members of the community typically have little money to improve the neighborhood and even less political clout to insist on a clean, healthy environment, poor citizens suffer the negative effects of a degraded environment to a greater extent than do affluent Americans or the middle class.
>
> *p. 46*

Certainly, this is true for the residents of Flint. The demographic indicators reveal Flint is a community vulnerable to environmental exposure.

Citizens Shut Out of Decision-Making Process

Residents were further shut out from democratic processes as a result of the State's emergency control of the City. The EM was not accountable to city council—and by extension citizens. According to Hammer (2019), they state that

> Flint residents had knowledge of the water crisis almost immediately upon the switch to the Flint River, but they lacked the power to influence the decision making of the Emergency Managers, Treasury, DEQ or the Governor (knowledge-&-power). This knowledge was real and visceral, flowing from the color, smell, taste and detrimental effects of the water on exposed skin. White community, complaints of residents based on this

knowledge alone would have forced change, because this knowledge would have combined with the power necessary to demand action.

p. 113

Environmental Injustice in Flint

Hammer (2019) goes on to explain how the disenfranchisement of Flint residents violated two important criteria central to environmental justice by stating that, environmental justice has both a procedural and a substantive component. Procedurally, environmental justice requires the ability of all people to participate in decision making regardless of race, color, national origin or income. Second, decisions must be substantively fair and non-discriminatory. By definition, Emergency Management violates the process criteria. In substance, it violated the second criterion. The Flint Water Crisis created a public health catastrophe that disproportionately affected people of color and other historically marginalized communities.

p. 113

Michigan's EM law has been challenged in federal court. Goodin-Smith (2019) explains that "plaintiffs argue that the law is unconstitutional because it disproportionately targets black communities and continues a narrative of structural and strategic racism" (p. 5). According to Hammer (2019), they state, "Structural racism consists of the inter-institutional dynamics that produce and reproduce rational disparate outcomes over time. These racially desperate outcomes occur in areas of health, education, income, transportation, housing and the environment" (p. 104). Hammer (2019) continues with, "Strategic racism is the conscious manipulation of the forces of intentional racism, structural racism and unconscious bias for economic or political gain. Structural racism creates the vulnerability and strategic racism exploits it" (p. 110). In this vein, Hammer (2019) asserts that the Flint Water Crisis is a story of strategic racism. He cites the initial decision for Flint to participate in the Karegnondi Water Authority (KWA), and the financially driven decision to use the Flint River as the interim drinking water source. As a part of the KWA, Flint was required to upgrade its waste water treatment plant, a financial endeavor it could not afford. Several alternative options were put forth early on; however, the EM structured the process to eliminate lower cost options so that the KWA commitment became the lowest cost scenario. Further, bond finance rules were manipulated to secure financing. Clearly a separate agenda was being served, and it was not out of the best interests, or even in consideration of Flint residents (Hammer, 2019, p. 111).

Moving Forward

Seven years after the Flint Water Crisis began, the City's resilience is on display as it strives to move forward even as thousands of children suffer the permanent effects of lead exposure (Washington Post, 2019). The switch back to Lake Huron water in 2015, coupled with the proper treatment of water to prevent corrosion of pipes, helped to prevent further lead contamination from the water as corrective action has taken place. A lawsuit filed by the Natural Resources Defense Council (NRDC, 2016) resulted in a 2017 court order mandating the inspection and replacement of lead service lines. As of June 2021, Flint is entering its final phase of removing lead water service lines (Detroit News, 2021). More than 27,000 water service lines have been checked, and 10,000 replaced. The initial investigation to hold officials accountable resulted in charges against eight individuals. However, in June 2019, prosecutors announced that they were dropping all criminal charges citing concerns about the investigative approach and legal theories used in the original investigation (Detroit Free Press, 2019). Criminal charges have since been refiled under the new state attorney general and prosecuting team. In January 2021, the State of Michigan announced the indictment of federal charges against 9 individuals, including the former Governor of Michigan, Rick Snyder, for a total of 42 counts related to a series of alleged actions and inactions. In the press conference to announce the charges, Michigan Solicitor General Fadwa Hammoud stated in State of Michigan (2021) that

> We must remember that the Flint Water Crisis is not some relic of the past. At this very moment, the people of Flint continue to suffer from the categorical failure of public officials at all levels of government, who trampled upon their trust, and evaded accountability for far too long. We understand that our work is not done and although the criminal justice system alone cannot remedy all the suffering that every person endured, we took our part seriously. We hope others will do the same to ensure this never, ever happens again.
>
> *State of Michigan, 2021, p. 2*

Looking Back: The Decline of Flint

The situation in Flint is a phenomenon that was several decades in the making. Asking "how did all of this happen" focuses on the present and doesn't look to the systemic matter in place. The first point is to look at when the decline happened in Flint. Flint was regarded as "Vehicle City," a place of prosperity for the middle-class worker in the automotive industry and a place where General Motors anchored its production. That anchoring by General Motors brings great opportunities, but that was the only opportunity and that is the problem. For a moment, let's compare Flint, Michigan, in the 1980s to Grand Rapids, Michigan, in 2019. Grand Rapids has a diverse economy that is not dependent or reliant upon one particular industry, so it should be able to adjust more effectively to economic fluctuations. Grand Rapids has furniture factories, breweries, a thriving hotel market, the "Medical Mile," and other thriving industries or components of its economy. Flint, Michigan, in the 1980s was heavily dependent or reliant upon the automotive industry. When that automotive industry left, as is famously depicted in the Michael Moore documentary "Roger and Me," much of the job market was gone in an instant (Moore et al., 1989; Rosner, 2016).

With the lack of economic opportunity, particularly among the city's poor African American population, there was a sharp increase in crime. In the period from the 1990s to 2019, the total number of violent crimes in Flint, Michigan, decreased, but the population declined by about 43,000 people or roughly 31%. More specifically, the number of homicides in Flint rose from about 40 homicides in 1995 to 60 homicides in 2020, while the population decreased by 43,000 people (Keefer & Murdock, 2020; US Department of Justice Federal Bureau of Investigation, 2019). Flint, like Detroit, faced the White Flight phenomenon in which economically advantaged whites fled to the suburbs or even outside of the Flint metropolitan statistical area altogether. As noted earlier in this chapter, Flint today is approximately 54% African American and has a poverty rate of roughly 42% overall (US Census Bureau, 2019). As crime rose and White Flight occurred, leading to population decline, the City of Flint collected less in tax revenue. Aging infrastructure was not replaced due to budgetary concerns, and this created the perfect storm for this type of environmental crisis (Brayman, 2016).

General Motors cut back jobs, which led to a rise in crime to offset a lack of economic opportunities for already marginalized communities of color. The economy began to dismantle, and businesses begin to flee the lack of opportunities and the rising crime. This led to foreclosures and a lack of tax revenues, which then compounded the situation as the municipal government's coffers emptied and infrastructure improvements, like replacing old lead water service lines, were delayed or ceased entirely to make up for budgetary shortfalls. The Flint Water Crisis did not begin overnight. It was a generation in the making.

Public Administration Theory and the Modern Political Environment

Around the 1980s with the ascension of Ronald Reagan to the presidency, the concept of Reaganomics emerged and was believed to be the American conception of the United Kingdom's Thatcherism. This belief that the private sector can do the work of the public sector more efficiently and effectively manifested through the concept known as the New Public Management. This body of thought emerged in the field of Public Administration through contracting out public services to private entities. In some areas, this may be true with waste management services being an example of a commonly implemented form of contracting out. One of the remarkable features of public administration and the democratic government of the United States in general is the implementation of measures that enhance accountability or checks and balances on systems in place.

Accountability deteriorated in Michigan with each amendment to or revision of emergency financial manager (EFM) laws, largely in an interest to rein in public spending in municipal governments with the general decline of the Michigan economy. This was compounded by the 2008 recession.

There are some instances of success with EFMs, like Detroit and Pontiac. However, the whole ideological backbone that supports the EFMs appears to be flawed in terms of accountability. The EFM laws of the 1980s, 1990s, and in the recent era with the Rick Snyder administration in Michigan created this "erosion of accountability" over time until it became a "malignant, cancerous growth" (Kasdan, 2014). Kasdan (2014) discusses "surviving cancer" with a comparison to EFMs and municipal government, emphasizing a return to "full recovery" for local governments that have an EFM replace democratically elected government for fiscal purposes (p. 1093). However, another type of "cancer" would be the type of cancer that the EFM system creates in terms of environmental justice and an overall lack of accountability. It is this "accountability cancer" that has poisoned the public dialogue on policy, and these beliefs that one EFM can make sound decisions over democratically elected public bodies have led to the Flint Water Crisis. Ironically, Kasdan (2014) was published in the same year as the start of the Flint Water Crisis.

The change over to the Flint River was meant to be a temporary solution in changing over to Lake Huron. It was a cost-effective measure that ignored social equity concerns of Public Administration. Is it possible that the Flint River could have been used safely? Yes, it is possible with appropriate treatment of the water and anti-corrosive treatment. The problem is that the Flint Emergency Financial Manager (EFM) looked at the situation through a cost-effective and efficiency lens and not a social equity lens. The basis for not using relatively cheap anti-corrosive water treatment is one that is void of rational, common sense. Lead leaching occurred because anti-corrosion treatment was not added to the water (Olson et al., 2017, p. 360). The relatively minimal cost of anti-corrosive water treatment compared to the millions of dollars in damages to property and infrastructure, healthcare costs of those that drank lead-tainted water, legal costs, and other attributable costs is a prime example of what happens when the "Fourth Pillar of Public Administration," social equity, is ignored by public administrators. Social equity is regarded as the "final frontier" of public administration due to largely complex systemic issues that seem to be "too large" for government to address (i.e., poverty, racism, and so on) (Frederickson, 2005; Frederickson, Smith, Larimer, & Licari, 2012; Gooden, 2015).

Environmental Injustice

The presence of Flint as the "Vehicle City" means factories that contribute to industrial pollution. The Flint River flows in a southwestern direction from Columbiaville, Michigan, meaning industrial pollution flows via contaminated water to the downtown Flint area. Additionally, there is roughly 100 years of chloride from road salt in the Flint River that passes through the downtown area, which is predominantly African American. The high levels of chloride in the Flint River made it corrosive, which created an environment of lead leaching from water pipes. This means that the chlorine levels dropped, which is believed to cause an environment habitable for Legionella, the bacteria that causes Legionnaire's Disease (Hersher, 2018).

Given White Flight and the environmental concerns with the Flint River, created an environment of "environmental racism," which means that African Americans and other minorities had a disparate environment to live in compared to Whites, given geographical and political considerations (Bullard, 2001). Additionally, the decision by the EFM at the time, Darnell Earley, to switch from the Detroit water system to the Flint River and to not provide for anti-corrosive treatment to the water given the Flint River's highly toxic contents created the crisis through lead leaching from the pipes. Earley's decision was ill-informed and there were no accountability measures in place (i.e., democratically elected council) to question the decision-making. In the aftermath, Earley and others were being charged with manslaughter and other criminal charges. However, the Attorney General Dana Nessel has dropped the criminal charges regarding the Flint Water Crisis at this point (Feldman, 2019).

Lack of Government Oversight

The EPA was created by the Nixon administration in 1969. One of the aspects of the EPA is to ensure that minorities are free from discrimination, through the enforcement of Title VI and the Civil Rights Act of 1964 as it relates to environmental policy. The legal landscape was enhanced in 1994 when President Bill Clinton signed an executive order to promote environmental justice for minorities. In the roughly 50 years since the EPA was formed and on the 25th anniversary of the environmental justice executive order, the findings by those who study the EPA's enforcement as it relates to protecting minorities is that the EPA has not substantially protected minorities because it has rejected numerous complaints, oftentimes on the basis of technicalities in the filing of such complaints. This has led to minorities experiencing disproportionately different environmental quality that has led to a measurable impact on the health of minorities, particularly African Americans and Hispanic Americans.

The Environmental Protection Agency and Environmental Injustice

The Flint Water Crisis is one of the major instances of environmental injustice in US history. Berliner (2017) defines that environmental injustice/racism is the disproportionately high level of risk to high-impact environmental hazards that certain communities or human groups, particularly people of color, in the United States face. As of 2014, 134 million US residents live within the "vulnerability" zones (estimates made by a facility of the maximum possible radius where people could be harmed by a worst-case release of certain toxic or flammable chemicals under EPA's Risk Management Planning program) (Berliner, 2017, p. 109). Furthermore, Berliner (2017) outlines the legal case that Flint residents have in their main claim is that defendants violated "Section 1983 because their actions unconstitutionally invaded upon the Flint residents' implied fundamental right to bodily integrity, as established by Substantive Due Process under the Fourteenth Amendment" (Berliner, 2017, p. 118).

The EPA, as part of the administrative branch of government, is required to fulfill constitutional obligations regarding the environment to ensure that all American citizens have equitable access to a clean environment. It is under the Fourteenth Amendment's "Substantive Due Process" and "Equal Protection of the Laws" provisions that President Clinton's environmental justice executive order can be fulfilled, but the EPA so far does not have a good track record and neither does the State of Michigan. The Flint Water Crisis was truly a failure of government at all levels. In CSPAN (2016a, 2016b, 2016c), one can see the different political parties place blame on one branch of government versus the other. Republicans want to blame the EPA, while Democrats want to blame the Republican Governor Rick Snyder and his administration. The Flint Water Crisis was a failure at every level of *administrative* government, exacerbated by political posturing.

There is some accountability for the Michigan state government officials that were involved in the Flint Water Crisis, pending judicial action. As of the 25th anniversary of Executive Order 12898, there is still much work to be done on the federal level. A court ruled that the EPA failed to protect civil rights by waiting a significant period of time to investigate civil rights complaints. According to the article, "Court declares that EPA failed to protect civil rights" (Yale University, 2018):

> In addition to the responsiveness and timeliness of the EPA, the Flint, Michigan residents are awaiting an update to the federal Lead and Copper Rule from the EPA, while they are making their case in the courts for environmental justice. As a concluding thought, why is it that the EPA has been able to ignore civil rights complaints with Executive Order 12898 in place? Does this Executive Order not seem to be enforceable? The initial civil rights complaint was in 1992, and it took 23 years for the courts to compel the EPA to follow the law. This is not a Public Administration that is accountable to the people that it serves. This Public Administration must increasingly focus on social equity.
>
> *Frederickson, 2005; Frederickson, Smith, Larimer,*
> *& Licari, 2012; Gooden, 2015*

Accountability

Criminally, nine former public officials have been charged, as of January 14, 2021, for their roles in the Flint Water Crisis. The nine former public officials include former Michigan Governor Rick Snyder, former Director of the Michigan Department of Health and Human Services, Nick Lyon, Governor Snyder's Senior Adviser Richard Baird, Governor Snyder's Chief of Staff and Vice President Pence's former Communications Director, Jarrod Agen, former Chief Medical Executive at MDHHS Dr. Eden Wells, former Flint Finance Director and appointed EFM Darnell Earley, former EFM Gerald Ambrose, former Flint Public Works Director Howard Croft, and Michigan's former Director of Maternal, Infant and Early Childhood Home Visiting, Nancy Peeler. Altogether, the nine public officials face 41 charges. Some argue that the charges for some, like former Governor Rick Snyder, are a light punishment because these charges are two misdemeanors with up to one year in jail or $1,000 fine. This is not exactly "justice" for a man who was once a CEO turned Governor (Guillen et al., 2021; LeBlanc & Mauger, 2021). In civil court, the US Supreme Court ruled that the residents of Flint could sue. Thus, there is a $640 million settlement for those in Flint who were subject to tainted lead water (Fletcher, 2020; LeBlanc & Mauger, 2021). While the financial settlement is appropriate in terms of civil court, it is not going to bring back a family member who died from Legionnaire's Disease. It does not address the fact that the water pipe fix will cost as much as $1.5 billion (Livengood, 2016).

Strategies for Achieving Resiliency

How would a city like Flint, Michigan, achieve resiliency? Crime is still not under control. Flint still has social injustices, even after the drinking water has returned to acceptable lead limits. There is still the persistent problem of the intersection of racial injustice and environmental injustice. The problem with Flint is that it can happen anywhere. The nation's infrastructure is crumbling. It is not unique to Flint (Ebert, 2021). To achieve resiliency, there must be a reengagement with the community to bring citizens into the decision-making process. There must be transparency in government decision-making, especially when it impacts residents. This level of trust was broken in Flint with the EM usurping democratic authority from the Flint City Council. Does one individual know better than an entire council whose members have been living in that community and are invested in that community?

It is important to have the proper structures in place to ensure that the Flint Water Crisis does not happen again. This would include continuous monitoring of lead levels in the drinking water. There should be a study to understand the current hazards by the past action to switch the drinking water over that led to the initial contamination. The oversight of Flint will need to include the formation of a citizen advisory board to assist the city in making informed decisions.

Discussion Questions

1. How can we learn from Flint? How might a social equity framework for Public Administration challenge public leadership to address systemic problems differently than in the past?
2. In what ways were public servants held accountable for Flint, and was it adequate? How would you hold a public servant accountable in such a large crisis as Flint?
3. Do you blame the State of Michigan or the EPA for the crisis in Flint? Do you blame both? Why?
4. How do you restore public confidence in the drinking water in Flint, which is now meeting EPA standards? How does this public health response relate to other public health challenges in modern times, such as getting the public to wear a mask or trust a coronavirus vaccine?
5. What does the roadmap look like for returning Flint to "greatness"? How does Flint reinvent itself, in both its public brand and its future?

References

ASPA Code of Ethics. (2016). Retrieved August 27, 2016, from www.aspanet.org/ASPA/About-ASPA/Code-of-Ethics/ASPA/Code-of-Ethics/Code-of-Ethics.aspx?hkey=fefba3e2-a9dc-4fc8-a686-3446513a4533.

Berliner, J.V. (2017). Environmental injustice/racism in Flint, Michigan: An analysis of the bodily integrity claim in Mays v. Snyder as compared to other environmental justice cases. Retrieved from https://digitalcommons.pace.edu/pelr/vol35/iss1/3.

Brayman, L. (2016, February 22). Why haven't Flint residents fled? Retrieved July 4, 2019, from www.washingtonpost.com/news/monkey-cage/wp/2016/02/22/why-havent-flint-.

Bullard, R. (2001, September). Confronting environmental racism in the 21st century. Retrieved August 26, 2016, from http://courses.arch.vt.edu/courses/wdunaway/gia5524/bullard.pdf.

Carmody,T. (2016). How the Flint River go so toxic.TheVerge. Retrieved from www.theverge.com/2016/2/26/11117022/flint-michigan-water-crisis-lead-pollution-history.

Centers for Disease Control and Prevention. (2021a). Blood lead levels in children. Centers for Disease Control and Prevention. Retrieved September 23, 2021, from www.cdc.gov/nceh/lead/prevention/blood-lead-levels.htm.

Centers for Disease Control and Prevention. (2021b). Childhood lead poisoning prevention. Retrieved September 15, 2021, from www.cdc.gov/nceh/lead/data/blood-lead-reference-value.htm.

CSPAN. (2016a, February 3). *Contaminated drinking water in Flint, Michigan.* [Video File]. Retrieved from www.c-span.org/video/?404078-1/hearing-contaminated-drinking-water-flint-michigan.

CSPAN. (2016b, March 15). *Flint, Michigan water contamination.* [Video File]. Retrieved from www.c-span.org/video/?406539-1/hearing-flint-michigan-water-contamination.

CSPAN. (2016c, March 17). *Flint, Michigan drinking water contamination.* [Video File]. Retrieved from www.c-span.org/video/?406540-1/hearing-flint-michigan-water-contamination.

Dana, D. A., & Tuerkheimer, D. (2017). After Flint: Environmental justice as equal protection. *Northwestern University Law Review*, 111(3), 879–890. Retrieved from http://search.ebscohost.com/login.aspx?direct=true&db=a9h&AN=122701835&site=ehost-live&scope=site.

Detroit Free Press. (2019). Why Michigan's Attorney General office wants a do-over in Flint. Retrieved from www.freep.com/story/opinion/columnists/brian-dickerson/2019/06/13/flint-water-investigation-do-over/1446870001/

Detroit News. (2021). Flint enters final stage of program removing lead water service lines. Retrieved from www.detroitnews.com/story/news/michigan/flint-water-crisis/2021/06/29/flint-enters-final-stage-program-removing-lead-water-service-lines/7802552002/.

Dixon, J. (2019). *How the crisis unfolded.* Detroit Free Press. Retrieved from www.freep.com/pages/interactives/flint-water-crisis-timeline/

Ebert, A. (2021, March 31). Flint serves as model and warning for Biden infrastructure plan. Bloomberg Law. https://news.bloomberglaw.com/environment-and-energy/flint-serves-as-model-and-warning-for-biden-infrastructure-plan.

Environmental Protection Agency. (2007). *National primary drinking water regulations for lead and copper: Short-term regulatory revisions and clarifications; final rule (to be codified at 40 C.F.R. Parts 141, 142).*

Environmental Protection Agency. (2019). Lead and copper rule. Retrieved from www.epa.gov/dwreginfo/lead-and-copper-rule.

Feldman, K. (2019, June 30). Flint prosecutors defend dropping charges against eight involved in water crisis. Retrieved from www.nydailynews.com/news/national/ny-flint-water-crisis-prosecutors-20190630-lsscymtlsfdhzdbbz3kvpujzu4-story.html.

Fletcher, S. (2020, December 1). The Flint water settlement and implications of the Michigan Supreme Court's reaffirmation of state constitutional tort claims. Retrieved January 14, 2021, from www.law.georgetown.edu/environmental-law-review/blog/the-flint-water-settlement-and-implications-of-the-michigan-supreme-courts-reaffirmation-of-state-constitutional-tort-claims/.

Frederickson, H. G. (2005, Winter). The state of social equity in American public administration. National Civic Review. Retrieved August 28, 2016 from, https://oied.ncsu.edu/selc/wp-content/uploads/2013/03/The-State-of-Social-Equity-in-American-Public-Administration.pdf.

Frederickson, H. G., Smith, K. B., Larimer, C. W., & Licari, M. J. (2012). *The public administration theory primer (2nd ed.).* Boulder, CO: Westview Press.

Gooden, S. T. (2015). From equality to social equity. In Guy, M. E. & Rubin, M. M., *Public administration evolving: From foundations to the future* (pp. 211–232). New York, NY: Routledge.

Goodin-Smith, O. (2019, January 30). Flint mayor wants state to give city control back to locals. Retrieved September 15, 2021, from www.mlive.com/news/flint/2018/01/its_time_for_flint_to_make_its.html.

Guillen, J., MacDonald, C., & Dixon, J. (2021, January 14). Ex-Gov. Rick Snyder pleads not guilty as nine face charges in Flint water crisis. Retrieved January 14, 2021, from www.freep.com/story/news/local/michigan/2021/01/14/rick-snyder-not-guilty-flint-water/4156962001/.

Hammer, P. J. (2019). The Flint water crisis, the Karegnondi Water Authority and strategic–structural racism. *Critical Sociology*, 45(1), 103–119. https://doi.org/10.1177/0896920517729193.

Hersher, R. (2018, February 05). Lethal pneumonia outbreak caused by low chlorine in Flint water. Retrieved July 4, 2019, from www.npr.org/sections/health-.

Kaffer, N. (2015). *Year before water change, state knew of risks in Flint*. Detroit Free Press. Retrieved from www.freep.com/story/opinion/columnists/nancy-kaffer/2015/11/07/flint-lead-water/75268692/

Kasdan, D. O. (2014). A tale of two hatchet men: Emergency financial management in Michigan. Retrieved from https://journals.sagepub.com/doi/abs/10.1177/0095399714554679.

Keefer, W., & Murdock, R. (2020, December 30). 'It's got to stop,' Flint community calls for end to gun violence after 4 killed over holiday weekend. Retrieved January 8, 2021, from www.mlive.com/news/flint/2020/12/its-got-to-stop-flint-community-calls-for-end-to-gun-violence-after-4-killed-over-holiday-weekend.html.

Krings, A., Kornberg, D., & Lane, E. (2018). Organizing under austerity: How residents' concerns became the Flint water crisis. *Critical Sociology*, 45(4/5), 583–597. https://doi.org/10.1177/0896920518757053.

Landrigan, P., & Bellinger, D. (2016, April 11). How to finally end lead poisoning in America. Time. Retrieved from https://time.com/4286726/lead-poisoning-in-america.

LeBlanc, B., & Mauger, C. (2021, January 14). Snyder, 8 others charged in Flint water probe: 'There are no velvet ropes'. Retrieved January 14, 2021, from www.detroitnews.com/story/news/local/michigan/2021/01/14/arraignments-begin-lyon-faces-involuntary-manslaughter-charges/4156464001/.

Livengood, C. (2016, January 8). Flint mayor: Water fix could cost as much as $1.5B. www.detroitnews.com/story/news/politics/2016/01/07/flint-water/78404218/.

Lotto Persio, S. (2018). Who is Leanne Walters? Activist who helped expose Flint water crisis wins top price. Newsweek. Retrieved from www.newsweek.com/who-leeanne-walters-activist-who-helped-expose-flint-water-crisis-wins-top-897326.

Martinez, J. (2016). *Environmental sustainability and American public administration*. Lanham, MD. Lexington Books.

Moore, M., Beaver, C., Prusak, J., Rafferty, K., Schermer, B., Stanzler, W., … Dog Eat Dog Films, Production Company. (1989). *Roger & me/Warner Bros. presents a Dog Eat Dog Films production; written, produced and directed by Michael Moore (25th anniversary edition; widescreen version ed.).* Los Angeles, CA: Warner Bros. Pictures.

National Public Radio. (2016). Lead-laced water in Flint: A step-by-step look at the makings of a crisis. Retrieved from www.npr.org/sections/thetwo-way/2016/04/20/465545378/lead-laced-water-in-flint-a-step-by-step-look-at-the-makings-of-a-crisis.

Natural Resources Defense Council. (2016). Case no. 16-10277. Retrieved from www.nrdc.org/sites/default/files/leg_16012701a.pdf.

Olson, T. M., Wax, M., Yonts, J., Heidecorn, K., Haig, S.-J., Yeoman, D., Hayes, Z., Raskin, L., & Ellis, B. R. (2017). Forensic estimates of lead release from lead service lines during the water crisis in Flint, Michigan. *Environmental Science & Technology Letters*, 4(9), 356–361. https://doi.org/10.1021/acs.estlett.7b00226.

Pieper, K. J., Tang, M., & Edwards, M. A. (2017). Flint water crisis caused by interrupted corrosion control: Investigating "ground zero" home. *Environmental Science & Technology*, 51(4), 2007–2014. Retrieved from https://pubs.acs.org/doi/10.1021/acs.est.6b04034.

Rosner, D. (2016). Flint, Michigan: A century of environmental injustice. *American Journal of Public Health*, 106(2), 200–201. Retrieved from http://libproxy.library.wmich.edu/login?url=https://www-proquest-com.libproxy.library.wmich.edu/scholarly-journals/flint-michigan-century-environmental-injustice/docview/1765549370/se-2?accountid=15099.

Sadler, R. C., LaChance, J., & Hanna-Attisha, M. (2017). Social and built environmental correlates of predicted blood lead levels in the Flint water crisis. *American Journal of Public Health*, 107(5), 763–769. https://doi.org/10.2105/AJPH.2017.303692.

Siddhartha, R. (2015). Flint River 19X more corrosive than Detroit water for lead solder; now what? Retrieved from http://flintwaterstudy.org/2015/09/page/3/.

Smith, L. (2015). After ignoring and trying to discredit people in Flint, the state was forced to face the problem. Michiganradio.org. Retrieved December 16, 2015, from www.michiganradio.org/post/after-ignoring-and-trying-discredit-people-flint-state-was-forced-face-problem#stream/0.

State of Michigan. (2011). Department of Treasury Communication. Retrieved from www.michigan.gov/documents/treasury/Flint-ReviewTeamReport-11-7-11_417437_7.pdf.

State of Michigan. (2016). Flint water advisory task force final report. Retrieved from www.michigan.gov/documents/snyder/FWATF_FINAL_REPORT_21March2016_517805_7.pdf.

State of Michigan. (2021). Nine indicted on criminal charges in Flint water crisis investigation. Retrieved from www.michigan.gov/som/0,4669,7-192-47796-549541--,00.html.

Stein, M. (1972, April). The Environmental Protection Agency and water quality control. *Natural Resources Lawyer*, 5(2), 237–248. Retrieved August 25, 2016, from www.jstor.org/stable/pdf/40921794.pdf.

US Census Bureau. (2018). Retrieved from www.census.gov/quickfacts/fact/table/flintcitymichigan/PST045218.

US Census Bureau. (2019). Flint City, Michigan QuickFacts. Retrieved July 4, 2019, from www.census.gov/quickfacts/table/PST045215/2629000.

US Department of Justice Federal Bureau of Investigation. (2019). Crime in the United States, 1995-2019. Retrieved January 7, 2021, from https://ucr.fbi.gov/crime-in-the-u.s.

Wakes, N. (2018). The Flint water crisis. *Anglican Theological Review*, 100(1), 143–145. Retrieved from http://search.ebscohost.com/login.aspx?direct=true&db=a9h&AN=127770226&site=ehost-live&scope=site.

Washington Post. (2019). How the Flint water crisis set back thousands of students. Retrieved from www.washingtonpost.com/education/2019/07/03/how-flint-water-crisis-set-back-thousands-students/.

Yale University. (2018, April 3). Court declares that EPA failed to protect civil rights. Retrieved July 15, 2019, from https://law.yale.edu/yls-today/news/court-declares-epa-failed-protect-civil-rights

5

ANTI-RESILIENCE FACTORS OF ENVIRONMENTAL JUSTICE COMMUNITIES

Janet A. Phoenix

Introduction

The Environmental Protection Agency (EPA) defines environmental justice as "fair and equal treatment in enforcement of environmental laws and regulations regardless of race, color, national origin or income…" (EPA, 2013). There are communities in the United States that have historically faced unequal treatment. Practices promoting segregated housing, disproportionate siting of toxic facilities, discrimination in access to quality education, and unequal treatment by governmental authorities who have not afforded their communities and residents the same protections have resulted in some communities experiencing environmental injustice or inequity. Many of those communities have higher numbers of African American and Hispanic residents and income levels are lower than surrounding communities not subject to the same environmental insults (Bullard et al., 2007; Taylor, 2014,).

This lack of fairness and equity in the past, and continued discriminatory practices in the present, may combine to work against the ability of communities of color to respond with resilience to environmental threats. To improve that resilience in these communities, an examination of the role each domain has had in promoting unfair environmental protections could assist in the effort to identify effective strategies to address them.

Resilience is defined as the "ability to bounce back after a jarring setback" (Dictionary by Merriam–Webster, 2021). For the purposes of this discussion, resilience is defined as the ability of environmental justice communities to respond effectively to threats and move in the direction of improved conditions and improved health for residents. Social and environmental factors can combine to negatively affect the ability of people living in environmental justice communities

DOI: 10.4324/9781003186076-6

to return to a state of health. Many factors may exert a combined effect on resilience, contributing to continued adversity, especially with respect to environmental quality. These include, but are not limited to, housing, education, the siting of polluting facilities/industries, and the political climate which can facilitate disproportionate siting of facilities that are potentially hazardous in environmental justice communities.

Housing

A legacy of housing discrimination practices has contributed to the isolation of ethnic minorities in segregated neighborhoods. Redlining, a practice of banks and other financial institutions refusing to grant housing loans to minorities who wish to purchase in geographic areas that are predominately white, has increased the concentration of minorities living in segregated communities by limiting their ability to purchase housing in communities that are majority white (Whittemore, 2017). Richard Rothstein in his novel, *The Color of Law*, described discriminatory lending practices that included special covenants in newly constructed communities that prohibited people of color from living with whites and made housing development construction funding contingent upon the enforcement of those covenants (Rothstein, 2017).

Zoning laws in some jurisdictions have been an additional mechanism contributing to segregation and an increased exposure to pollution. Permitting processes that enabled industrial facilities, waste processing plants, highways, and other potentially toxic facilities to be located in segregated minority communities have helped to render the places where ethnic minorities/low-income people lived less desirable (Whittemore, 2017). This also made the possibility of reselling properties in these communities more challenging. When resales did occur, lower property values often limited the ability of property owners to have the purchasing power to move to areas of the city where exposure to pollution was less likely. These zoning practices also helped to ensure that housing in these neighborhoods would be considered less desirable, branding ethnic minority communities as inferior (Rothstein, 2017).

City planning and discriminatory zoning practices can have long-lasting effects, encouraging the continued siting of polluting facilities in these neighborhoods. Once people have lived in a neighborhood for a long time, the social connections they have formed and the establishments and institutions they are accustomed to discourage migration. Groups of people tend to stay where they are, and many historical segregated housing patterns are with us today (Rothstein, 2015, 2017).

The obstacles that purchasers of color face when trying to secure financing to obtain homes in neighborhoods that are predominately white also apply to renters of color. Renters face similar obstacles in viewing and renting properties in majority white neighborhoods. Minorities continue to be steered to neighborhoods that are in predominantly minority communities perpetuating segregated housing practices (Taylor, 2014).

Education

One measure of disparities in education is scoring on standardized measures of reading and mathematics. In the United States, there are gaps in reading and math between African American and Caucasian students, with Caucasian students scoring higher on assessments. Caucasian students complete more higher level mathematics courses. The percentage of African American children earning advanced placement or international baccalaureate credit was lower than for Caucasian children (US Department of Education, 2018).

Neighborhoods where minorities are predominant often have overcrowded poor-quality schools (Atlantic, 2021; Brookings Institute, 1998). A consequence of these educational disparities in neighborhoods where adverse environmental exposures are more common may be fewer children who are adequately prepared to interpret data that illustrates the risk posed by polluting facilities in their neighborhoods and to understand and articulate the increased exposures that result from these (Rothstein, 2015).

This has the potential to reduce the number of residents in environmental justice communities who are able to interpret what data exists documenting exposures, leaving communities more vulnerable. Governmental agencies and representatives may communicate information in ways that are not commonly used by residents of environmental justice communities. For example, notices may be posted in news publications or on websites not regularly used by affected communities. This may result in community members receiving information about time-sensitive activities such as hearings too late to be able to respond. Reports that are released for public comment may be written in technical language and/or at a high reading level or in language that cannot be understood by affected community members. The Executive Order (12898) on environmental justice laid out a framework promoting broader public participation for low-income and minority communities as part of an environmental justice strategy. Strategies implemented by EPA to enforce the order called for measures to increase participation through the use of documents that are easy to understand and translation of material into other languages when appropriate (EPA, 2021a). Sharing highly technical environmental information about environmental exposures without making an adequate effort to ensure they are understood may not answer questions that community residents have about what potential exposures can result from the siting of a facility in their neighborhood or what it will mean for their health and the health of their families. "The mechanisms through which neighborhoods have an impact on future outcomes for their residents…likely results from the lack of political power and access to public resources and institutions that often comes with residence in a low-income neighborhood" (Shindler, 2015).

As racial barriers to housing purchase and renting have become more porous with the passage of the Fair Housing Act, a pattern of migration has emerged that is troubling to the author. Higher educated, wealthier minority community members have moved out of segregated highly polluted communities in higher numbers, than their less well educated, lower income counterparts. This has left many communities racially and economically segregated when before they had been economically mixed and more resilient. This pattern has increased the vulnerability of these communities because there are fewer community members remaining who can interpret data on exposures, navigate the political system, and advocate effectively for improved conditions (Taylor, 2014).

Political Indifference

The political institutions that are in place to protect communities are not free of bias. Economic wealth and race factor into decision-making processes that affect housing construction, housing code enforcement, environmental rulemaking, and a host of other decisions that affect the health and well-being of communities of color (Rothstein, 2017; Taylor, 2014). A social cost that flows from the legacy of segregation in housing is that inferior social status can be reinforced through a lack of political will to address environmental inequities. Isolation in low-income communities can "… engender their absence from valuable social {and political} networks" (Shindler, 2015).

Siting of Polluting Facilities in Poor/Minority Neighborhoods

While the Fair Housing Act of 1968 eliminated the legal framework for housing discrimination, it did little to change zoning practices that contributed to the continued location of toxic facilities in communities of color and low-income communities. Toxic Waste and Race, a seminal work by Dr. Robert Bullard, detailed patterns of disproportionate siting of toxic facilities in low-income and minority communities. The United Church of Christ also helped to map the location of toxic facilities using a zip code analysis. Zip codes that were predominately African American or Hispanic were more likely to contain toxic facilities (Bullard et al., 2007).

Power plants, municipal waste facilities, highways, and other industrial facilities are examples of these kinds of facilities that were found to be more common in communities with higher numbers of African American and Hispanic residents. The following examples illustrate this pattern of location and toxic exposure for the communities.

Environmental Justice in the Nation's Capital

Many municipalities in the United States have communities where historical segregation, zoning practices, and location of toxic facilities occur in environmental justice communities. The nation's capital is no exception. The nation's capital was at one time home to the Benning Power Plant. Power generating activities at the plant ceased on June 1, 2012. The buildings and equipment that had been used to generate power were dismantled in May 2015 (Benning Service Center, 2022). The site remains as a power transfer facility and has been operated by Pepco Energy Services since 2000. For many years, the Benning Power Plant operated as a coal-fired power plant in a densely populated urban community, with more than 90% of its population African American residents. The Pepco Benning Road facility is located at 3400 Benning Road NE, Washington, DC and sits on approximately 77-acres. The site is bordered by the District Department of Public Works (DPW) Solid Waste Transfer Station. This site operated as an incinerator from 1972 to 1994. Approximately 1000 tons of waste per day was incinerated during the operating hours (24 hours a day, 5 days per week). There are residential areas to the east and south of the site. The site also borders on the Langston Golf course, a historically Black golf course, and to a former site of a municipal waste incineration facility for the District of Columbia. The Kenilworth Landfill site is the east of the power plant. This landfill is no longer accepting waste but was formerly the repository for waste for the city. The former Kenilworth landfill is now known as Kenilworth Park and Aquatic Gardens, a site managed by the National Park Service (Pepco, 2019).

A Community Advisory Group (CAG) has been meeting monthly with power company representatives, civic association and neighborhood representatives as well as representatives of the District of Columbia Department of Energy and the Environment as part of a Remedial Investigation and Feasibility Study (RI/FS) to determine an appropriate cleanup plan for the site. This has been an effective tool for allowing the community to receive information about the project and to dialogue with PEPCO staff and staff from the DC Department of the Environment. As part of a voluntary consent decree, Pepco agreed to "assess the nature and extent of contamination and any threat to the public health, welfare and environment caused by releases or threatened releases from the facility." Pepco also agreed to "identify and evaluate alternatives designed to remediate or mitigate release of hazardous substances, pollutants or contaminants" from the Benning Road facility through a feasibility study (US District Court for the District of Columbia, 2011).

This work has been undertaken as a collaborative effort to increase the participation of the public in environmental policy-making and could serve as a model for other communities. Neighborhood residents will have a role in determining what measures should be implemented to address chemicals left behind in soil, groundwater, and the Anacostia River. The CAG is focused specifically on the impact of the power plant. Many community members, however, acknowledge that other chemical exposures have occurred in the past and that the communities adjacent to the Benning Service Center have been at the epicenter of many exposures from many sources including the landfill, the highway, and other sites in close proximity to the plant (ATSDR, 2005).

The Community

The community immediately surrounding the PEPCO Benning Service Center includes the neighborhoods Deanwood, Eastland Gardens, Kenilworth Parkside, Kingman Park, Marshall Heights, Mayfair and River Terrace. The people living in these neighborhoods have a range of incomes and educational levels. When some neighborhoods, however, are compared with the city as a whole they are below average on certain demographic and social indicators. For example, Eastland Gardens has a lower life expectancy and a higher percentage of residents with low income levels compared to the city as a whole. Marshall Heights has higher unemployment rates and more residents are spending a high percentage of their income on rent when compared with the city as a whole (DC Health, 2018). There are approximately 75,000 people living in Ward 7 where the plant is located (DC Health Matters, 2021). The District of Columbia has a concentration in the eastern and southern parts of the city of minority low-income residents. The north and western sections of the city have fewer minority residents and income levels are higher (DC Health Matters, 2021). Asthma emergency room visits are highest in Wards 7 and 8 (Children's National, 2022). The District of Columbia as a whole has outcomes worse than the nation for asthma, HIV, stroke, and infant mortality. Unemployment rates in Wards 7 and 8 are 19% and 17%, respectively, compared with 3.4% for Ward 3, the ward that has the highest income and the highest percentage of Caucasian residents (DC Department of Health, 2014, DC Health Matters, 2021).

Wards 7 and 8, the sections of the District of Columbia closest to the power plant, the trash transfer facility and the former landfill, have higher numbers of African American residents than the city as a whole. Health indicators for life expectancy, asthma emergency room visits, cardiovascular disease, cancer, and other outcomes are poorer in Wards 7 and 8 than in wards of the city with higher numbers of Caucasian residents and higher incomes (DC Department of Health, 2018). Wards 7 and 8 have a lower mean age compared with the city as a whole, indicating larger numbers of children (DC Department of Health, 2018).

There is one hospital located in this section of the city, United Medical Center (Street Sense Media, 2019). A high traffic corridor (Route 295) runs through the affected neighborhoods adding gasoline combustion byproducts to other pollutants (DC Department of Transportation, 2022). Access to parks and play spaces is limited, so all of these neighborhoods have been characterized as scoring low on an index of environmental health (Rand, 2009). Environmental justice is a term that has been used to describe neighborhoods that are predominately low-income and/or minority and where environmental quality is poor (EPA, 2013). That term would seem to apply to the neighborhoods in Northeast Washington near the former coal-fired power plant, the former landfill, the trash facility and the current high-traffic transportation corridor. The cumulative impact on the neighborhood and the health of the residents from the legacy left behind by the past exposures combined with ongoing exposure has yet to be fully evaluated.

Air Pollution Linked to Respiratory Diseases Like Asthma

There is evidence linking exposure to traffic related air pollutants (TRAP) to exacerbations of respiratory diseases like asthma. The list of pollutants includes particulate matter, volatile organic compounds, some criteria air pollutants (EPA, 2022), and also polycyclic aromatic hydrocarbons (PAHs) produced by combustion byproducts from motor vehicles (Cortessis et al., 2012; Hong et al., 2016). Power plants can be another source of PAHs found in the environment (Alegbeyele et al., 2017). There is also growing evidence that epigenetic mechanisms including DNA methylation and modification of histones may be influenced by air pollution (Cortessis et al., 2012). These effects of exposure may occur in adults, in young children, and in fetuses (Yang & Schwartz, 2012). This has important implications because epigenetic modifications have the potential to span generations. This could mean that exposure to pollution in one generation has the potential to pre-dispose the next generation to the development of diseases such as asthma, cancer, neurological diseases, and metabolic diseases like diabetes and obesity (Cortessis et al., 2012). Future research may reveal the nature and extent of this potential impact, shedding light on the relationship between past exposure to environmental air pollutants and respiratory disease in the offspring of those exposed. This has implications for the resilience of environmental justice communities who may continue to experience the consequences of past chemical exposures for many generations to come.

Contamination from Coal-Fired Plants

Coal-fired power plants have been associated with exposures to many chemicals with adverse health effects (Hagemeyer et al., 2019). Some of the exposures may be the result of the combustion products of coal that are released into the atmosphere through the stacks (Panda et al., 2015). Exposure to these chemicals is associated with asthma, allergies, and other lung diseases. Some exposures result from chemicals generated during the industrial process to convert energy from coal into electricity. The combustion of coal creates coal ash which can contain heavy metals and PAHs (Alegbeleye et al., 2017; Hagemeyer et al., 2019). Two chemical families, in particular polychlorinated biphenyls (PCBs) and PAHs, are a concern because of their toxicity (Alegbeleye et al., 2017; Perrera et al., 2011).

Landfills and Incinerators

Landfills are used to dispose of waste in urban settings. The process of inciner-ation can reduce waste volume and slow or eliminate the spread of pathogens that may be present in the waste. There is also the potential to harness thermal energy to generate electricity (Reeve et al., 2013). Landfills in the United States and Europe have been shown to be more likely to be located in close proximity to communities where income and educational levels are lower when compared with communities of higher income and educational levels (Martuzzi et al., 2010). Landfills and incinerators can have an adverse effect on property values depending upon the size of the facility and the volume of waste (Taylor, 2014).

Chemical Contaminants Associated with Power Plants, Incinerators, and Landfills

The following chemicals are often emitted into the air, soil, or groundwater from power generating plants, incinerators, and/or landfills. Each of these chemical families have health effects associated with them, but those effects can sometimes combine leading to synergistic and cumulative impacts that are difficult to quantify or estimate. For environmental justice communities that are close to multiple emitting facilities, the ability to preserve the health and well-being of their residents may be challenged not only by social factors but also by the lack of accessible, credible information that informs them about the combined risks they face.

Polycyclic Aromatic Hydrocarbons (PAHs)

PAHs are produced when combustion doesn't fully destroy the fuel source. The burning of coal, oil, or garbage can produce PAHs. These compounds can be found in soil, groundwater, drinking water, and food. PAHs can bind to the genetic material and proteins in living things. They have the potential to cause cancer and affect early childhood development. It is difficult to link specific health effects to a specific compound in the PAH family. When you are exposed, it is usually to more than one compound. Preexisting conditions and other factors like age or youth can influence the toxicity resulting from exposure to PAHs. Exposure to other pollutants at the same time that you are exposed to PAHs can make the effects worse (Alegbeleye et al., 2017). School children in New York with higher levels of PAHs in their cord blood samples scored higher scores on tests of anxiety, depression, and attention at ages 7 and 8 (Perera et al., 2011).

PAHs can be found in the soil after settling out of the air near industrial sites where they are formed. Industries linked to this kind of exposure include waste incinerators and power generating facilities. Urban roadways are also a source of soil contamination, particularly roads close to airports and highways. Water contamination results from the deposition of particles and vapors can form part of runoffs especially near industrial facilities. Wastewater discharges and oil spills are a source of water contamination (Alegbeleye et al., 2017). Urban roadways can be a source of exposure due to atmospheric pollution from the incomplete combustion of fossil fuels used in automobiles and trucks (Perera et al., 2011). PAHs can bind to DNA and proteins in cells resulting in mutations, potentially leading to cancer and developmental disorders (Alegbeleye et al., 2017).

Polychlorinated Biphenyls (PCBs)

PCBs are mixtures of up to 209 individual compounds and can persist in fat tissue and soil. There are no known natural sources of PCBs. They were used in a variety of industrial and commercial products. PCBs were domestically manufactured from 1929, until their manufacture was banned in 1979 (ATSDR, 2000, 2011, 2012; EPA, 2021b). PCBs can last a long time in the environment. They can be found in air, water, and soil. PCBs are sometimes found in the bodies of small animals and fish. People who fish for food may be exposed to PCBs that are stored in the fish (ATSDR, 2000; EPA, 2021b). Old electrical devices may contain PCBs if they were made before PCB use was halted. When electric devices get hot during operation, small amounts of PCBs may get into the air. Because devices that contain PCBs can leak with age, they could also be a source of skin exposure to PCBs (ATSDR, 2000). The list of potential health effects is long. There are potential effects on many body systems including the nervous system, reproductive system, and endocrine system. PCBs are believed to cause cancer in humans (ATSDR, 2000; EPA, 2021b). Women who are exposed to PCBs during pregnancy are at risk of having children with low birth weight (ATSDR, 2000; EPA, 2021b). PCBs can be toxic to the neurological system and in children adverse health effects include decreased cognitive function, memory, and executive function. Because PCBs can enter the waste stream when old devices are thrown away, the exposure can potentially be more widespread than to people directly exposed to industrial uses (Chen et al., 2011).

Metals

Metals can be found in landfills and may be contaminants found near incinerators. Metals are released into the environment as components of electronic and other waste and can travel beyond waste facilities as particles emitted from smokestacks, from the incineration of waste and through leaching into soil and groundwater (Chen et al., 2011; Jashankar et al., 2014; Mattiello et al., 2013). Following are examples of metals in the waste stream and the health effects associated with them.

Mercury

Mercury is a naturally occurring metal that has several forms. When mercury combines with carbon to make organic mercury compounds it takes a form (methylmercury) that can have the most serious health effects (ATSDR, 1999; EPA, 2021c). Human beings can be exposed to mercury when they breathe contaminated air from a spill. People can also eat food or drink water that contains mercury contamination (ATSDR 1999; EPA, 2021c). Eating fish or shellfish is the most common way that people in the United States are exposed to mercury

(ATSDR, 1999; EPA, 2021c). Some mercury-containing products may enter the waste stream. Mining, industrial wastewater discharges, incineration, and pulp and paper industries can be sources of mercury in the environment (Jashankar et al., 2014).

The list of potential health effects from mercury includes irritability, tremors, changes in vision or hearing, memory problems, skin rashes, and eye irritation. Mercury can damage the brain, kidneys, and developing fetuses. The nervous system is very sensitive to all forms of mercury (EPA, 2021c). Mercury vapors are associated with asthma, bronchitis, and other respiratory effects (Jashankar et al., 2014).

Pregnant women with elevated mercury levels can give birth to children with neurological defects (Jashankar et al., 2014). Very young children are more sensitive to mercury than adults. Mercury in the mother's body can pass to the developing fetus and can also pass to a nursing infant through breast milk. Mercury's harmful effects on children exposed before birth can include brain damage, lack of coordination, blindness, seizures, and inability to speak (ATSDR, 1999; EPA, 2021c).

Lead

Lead can enter the waste stream through discarded televisions and computer monitors. It is used as a solder in circuit boards (Chen et al., 2011). Lead is also used in batteries and pipes that carry drinking water and in some manufacturing processes (Jashankar et al., 2014). Older residences built before 1978 may contain lead-based paints. This paint can deteriorate resulting in lead exposure in the dust (Health Impact Project, 2017). Building components containing lead can enter the waste stream. Lead can be inhaled or ingested. Very small amounts of lead can poison a child or an adult. Small children are exposed to lead when they touch leaded surfaces and put their hands in their mouths. Lead dust can cling to the hands and children can swallow small particles or leaded dust leading to higher levels of lead in their blood (Lanphear et al., 1997).

Lead affects the development of children's brains and nervous systems. They can lose intelligence quotient (IQ) points and experience learning and attention deficits e.g. hyperactivity. Lead changes the way children learn affecting information processing and on a population basis, can cause groups of children who are exposed to have lower rates of graduation from school and higher rates of incarceration (Chen et al., 2011; Health Impact Project, 2017).

Summary of Concerns about Health Effects from Environmental Chemicals

Because some low-income and minority communities are more likely to be near facilities like incinerators, landfills, and transportation corridors, they may experience more exposure to the chemicals discussed earlier. Each family of chemicals has its' own set of potential effects but what is concerning is the overlap of the potential health effects of these chemicals, especially for pregnant women and children.

PCBs and PAHs have been associated with neurological effects in children (ATSDR, 2000; Chen et al., 2011; EPA, 2021b). Exposure to metals like mercury and lead can reduce cognitive abilities and increase antisocial behavior in children (EPA, 2021c; Health Impact Project, 2017). Reproductive effects such as low birth weight as well as developmental effects on the nervous system are also linked to PCB exposure (ATSDR, 2000; EPA, 2021b). For families with young children living near landfills, incinerators, and high traffic transportation corridors, there may be multiple sources of exposure that can negatively impact the neurological development of children.

Exposure to PAHs can contribute to increased rates of asthma and other respiratory diseases increasing the risk for people living close to roadways and polluting facilities (Alegbeyele et al., 2017). Coal-fired power plants, landfills, and incinerators are all linked to higher environmental exposure for these chemicals (Hagemeyer et al., 2019; Martuzzi et al., 2010; Mattielo et al., 2013).

Environmental justice communities are more likely to have clusters of polluting facilities nearby (Bullard et al., 2007). Little work has been done to estimate the cumulative effects of this exposure and the potentially augmented effect of multiple chemical exposures.

When multiple pollution sources combine the potential for this to enhance the adverse impacts on the health of people living nearby is not yet clear, but may be substantial. When you combine the potential overlapping effects of chemical exposure with social determinants that can adversely affect health, such as housing and education, the ability of environmental justice communities to be resilient to these environmental threats may be limited.

Conclusion

The factors of housing, lack of mobility, disproportionate siting of toxic facilities, lower quality education, and political indifference can combine to isolate environmental justice communities and increase their exposure to potentially harmful chemicals. People who live in segregated communities are more likely to live where housing quality is poor and are subjected to environmental contaminants inside their homes as well as in the neighborhoods that surround them (Bullard et al, 2007).

Toxic facilities such as power plants, landfills, and incinerators are more likely to receive permits to locate in environmental justice communities. This can start a cascade effect leading to additional facilities being located in communities where similar facilities have been located in the past. There may be little political will to disapprove these permits or plan for potentially polluting facilities to locate in wealthier communities with fewer residents of color because constituents living in environmental justice communities may not wield the same influence as other constituents.

The impacts of the presence of facilities that emit toxic chemicals into the air, soil, and groundwater are difficult to evaluate. Despite our inability to quantify these risks, there is mounting evidence that the effects may be cumulative from multiple sources. It is becoming clearer that many of the potential health effects from exposure to these chemicals overlap by targeting the same critical pathways.

Neurological damage, poor birth outcomes, cancer, metabolic disease, and long-term behavioral changes such as antisocial behavior may share environmental determinants that are common to the environments of environmental justice communities. These factors can combine with social determinants to sap the resilience and limit the ability of communities to respond to continued environmental threats. They may also inhibit the ability of people living in the communities to ameliorate the effects because their ability to access better quality housing and environmentally safer communities is diminished. The impacts of adverse environmental exposures do not have to be pervasive or long lasting. In the case of lead, evidence suggests that when pathways of exposure are interrupted early and when children are identified and supported in home and educational settings, they can go on to achieve at levels that are comparable to their counterparts who were not exposed (Pew, 2017). This suggests that it is possible for environmental justice communities to become more resilient if they have access to resources such as quality education, safe and affordable housing, clean air and water, and an equitable environmental policy framework.

Yet, in environmental justice communities across the United States, access to those resources seems to be diminishing, and the disparities in environmental quality appear to be widening. Some communities appear to becoming less well educated and poorer. This may limit the resilience of such communities to protect themselves from the adverse environmental conditions that have come to exemplify environmental justice.

Discussion Questions

1. What kinds of social factors contribute to environmental exposure for low-income/minority people in the United States?
2. What does the term resilience mean as it is applied to environmental justice communities?
3. The Executive Order (12898) for environmental justice was designed to promote public participation in environmental decision-making; what actions can localities and states take to make this happen?
4. Is it a single chemical exposure or the long-term exposure to multiple chemicals that is most problematic for environmental justice communities?

References

Agency for Toxic Substances and Disease Registry (ATSDR). (1999). Toxicological Profile for Mercury. US Department of Health and Human Services Public Health Service. Retrieved October 2021 from www.atsdr.cdc.gov/toxprofiles/tp46.pdf.

Agency for Toxic Substances and Disease Registry (ATSDR). (2000). Toxicological Profile for Polychlorinated Biphenyls. US Department of Health and Human Services Public Health Service. Retrieved October 2021 from www.atsdr.cdc.gov/ToxProfiles/tp68.pdf.

Agency for Toxic Substances and Disease Registry (ATSDR). (2005). Public Health Assessment for River Terrace Community, Washington, DC. July 21, 2005. US Department of Health and Human Services. Retrieved October 2021 from http://benningservicecenter.com/library/documents/ATSDRPublicHealthAssessment.pdf.

Agency for Toxic Substances and Disease Registry (ATSDR). (2011). The Priority List of Hazardous Substances. Retrieved from www.atsdr.cdc.gov/spl/index.html. Accessed September 1, 2021.

Agency for Toxic Substances and Disease Registry (ATSDR). (2012). Dioxins and Furans. www.epa.gov/osw/hazard/wastemin/minimize/factshts/dioxfura.pdf.

Alegbeleye, O., Oluwatoyin, B., & Jackson, V.A. (2017). Polycyclic Aromatic Hydrocarbons: A Critical Review of Environmental Occurrence and Bioremediation. *Environmental Management, 60*(4): 758–783. https://doi.org/10.1007/.

Atlantic. (February 29, 2016). The Concentration of Poverty in American Schools. Retrieved October 2, 2021 from www.theatlantic.com/education/archive/2016/02/concentration-poverty-american-schools/471414/

Benning Service Center: Power Closure. (2022). Retried February 15, 2022 from www.benningservicecenter.com/benning-power-plant-closure

Brookings Institute. (March 1, 1998). Unequal Opportunity: Race and Education. Retrieved October 2, 2021 from www.brookings.edu/articles/unequal-opportunity-race-and-education/.

Bullard, R.D., Mohai, P., Saha, R., Wright, B. (2007). Toxic Waste and Race at 20: 187–2007. United Church of Christ, Justice and Witness Ministries.

Chen, A., Dietrich, K.N., Huo, X., & Ho, S. (2011). Developmental Neurotoxicants in E-Waste: An Emerging Health Concern. *Environmental Health Perspectives, 119*: 431–438. Doi:10.1289/ehp.1002452.

Children's National. (2022). IMPACT DC Improving Pediatric Asthma Care in the District of Columbia. Retrieved February 2022 from http://childrensnational.org/departments/impact-dc-asthma-clinic.

Cortessis, V.K., Thomas, D.C., Levine, A.J., Breton, C.V., Mack, T.M., Siegmund, K.M., Haile, & Laird, P.W. (2012). Environmental Epigenetics: Prospects for Studying Epigenetic Mediation of Exposure-Response Relationships. *Human Genetics, 131*: 1365–1389.

DC Health Matters. (2021). Ward 7 Demographic Data. Retrieved October 2021 from www.dchealthmatters.org/demographicdata?id=131494.

Dictionary by Merriam-Webster. (2021). Resilience. Retrieved October 2021 from www.merriam-webster.com/.

District of Columbia Department of Health. (2014). Community Health Needs Assessment Volume I. Retrieved October 2021 from https://dchealth.dc.gov/sites/default/files/dc/sites/doh/page_content/attachments/DC%20DOH%20CHNA%20%28v5%200%29%2005%2007%202014%20-%20FINAL%20%282%29.pdf.

District of Columbia Department of Health. (2018). Health Equity Report: The Social and Structural Determinants of Health. Office of Health Equity, District of Columbia Department of Health.

District of Columbia Department of Transportation. (2022). Interstate 295/Malcolm X Interchange Improvements. Retrieved February 15, 2022 from: https://ddot.dc.gov/ page/interstate-295-malcolm-x-interchange-improvements.

Environmental Protection Agency. (2013). Environmental Justice Terms As Defined Across the PSC Agencies. Retrieved October 2021 from www.epa.gov/sites/production/files/ 2015-02/documents/team-ej-lexicon.pdf.

Environmental Protection Agency. (2021a). Fact Sheet on the Environmental Justice Executive Order. Retrieved September 29, 2021 from www.epa.gov/environmental justice/factsheet-epas-office-environmental-justice

Environmental Protection Agency. (2021b). Learn about Polychlorinated Biphenyls. Retrieved October 2021 from www.epa.gov/pcbs/learn-about-polychlorinated-biphenyls-pcbs#commercial.

Environmental Protection Agency. (2021c). Basic Information about Mercury. Retrieved September 2021 from www.epa.gov/mercury/basic-information-about-mercury; retrieved October 2021 from www.epa.gov/fedfac/epa-insight-policy-paper-executive-order-12898-environmental-justice.

Environmental Protection Agency. (2022). Criteria Air Pollutants. Retrieved February 2022 from www.epa.gov/criteria-air-pollutants.

Hagemeyer, A.N., Sears, C.G., & Zierold, K.M. (2019). Respiratory Health in Adults Living Near a Coal Burning Power Plant with Coal Ash Storage Facilities: A Cross Sectional Epidemiological Study. *International Journal of Environmental Research and Public Health*, *16*: 3642.

Health Impact Project. (2017). 10 Policies to Prevent and Respond to Childhood Lead Exposure: An Assessment of the Risks Communities Face and Key Federal, State and Local Solutions. Health Impact Project, Pew Charitable Trusts. Retrieved May 2020 from www.pewtrusts.org/-/media/assets/2017/08/hip_childhood_lead_poisoning_ report.pdf.

Hong, J., Myers, J.M., Brandt, E.B., Brokamp, C., Ryan, P.H., & Hershey, G.K. (2016). Air Pollution, Epigenetics and Asthma. *Allergy, Asthma & Clinical Immunology*, *12*: 51.

Jashankar, M., Tseten, T., Anbalagan, N., Mathew, D., & Beeregowda, K. (2014). Toxicity, Mechanisms and Health Effects of Some Heavy Metals. *Interdisciplinary Toxicology*, *7*(2): 60–72.

Lanphear, B. P., & Roghmann, K. J. (1997). Pathways of Lead Exposure in Urban Children. *Environmental Research*, 74: 67–73.

Martuzzi, M., Mitis, F., & Forastiere, F. (2010). Inequalities, Inequities, Environmental Justice in Waste Management and Public Health. *European Journal of Public Health*, *20*(1): 21–26.

Mattiello, A., Chiodini, P., Bianco, E., Forgione, N., Flammia, I., Gallo, C., Pizzuiti, R., & Panico, S. (2013). Health Effects Associated with the Disposal of Solid Waste in Landfills and Incinerators in Populations Living in Surrounding·Areas: A Systematic Review. *International Journal of Public Health*, *58*: 725–735.

Panda, B.B., Kumar, A., Bhattacharyya, P., Bardhan, G., Gupta, S., & Patra, D.K. (2015). Impairment of Soil Health due to Fly Ash Fugitive Dust Deposition from Thermal Coal Fired Power Plant. *Environmental Monitoring and Assessment*, *187*: 679.

Perera, F., Wang, S., Vishnevetsky, J., Zhang, B., Cole, K., Tang, D., Rauh, V., & Phillips, D. (2011). Polycyclic Aromatic Hydrocarbons-Aromatic DNA Adducts in Cord Blood and Behavior Scores in New York City Children. *Environmental Health Perspectives*, *119*: 1176–1181.

The Pew Charitable Trusts. (August 2017). A Report from the Health Impact Project. 10 Policies to Prevent and Respond to Childhood Lead Exposure: An Assessment of the Risks Communities Face and Key federal, State and Local Solution.

Potomac Electric Power Company (PEPCO). (2019). Remedial Investigation and Feasibility Study Draft Final. Retrieved October 2021 from http://benningservicecenter.com/library/documents/Remedial-Investigation-Report-Draft-Final-September-2019.pdf

Rand Health. (2009). Health and Healthcare among District of Columbia Youth. The Rand Corporation supported by Children's National Medical Center. Library of Congress 978-0-8330-4805-9.

Reeve, N.F., Fanshawe, T.R., Keegan, T.J., Stewart, A.G., & Diggle, P.J. (2013). Spatial Analysis of Health Effects of Large Industrial Incinerators in England 1998-2008, a Study Using Matched Case Control Areas. *BMJ Open*, *3*(1).

Rothstein, R. (2015). The Racial Achievement Gap, Segregated Schools, and Segregated Neighborhoods – A Constitutional Insult. *Race and Social Problems*, *7*(1): 21–30.

Rothstein, R. (2017). The Color of Law: A Forgotten History of How Our Government Segregated America. Liveright. ISBN: 9781631492853.

Shindler, S. (2015). Architectural Exclusion: Discrimination and Segregation through Physical Design of the Built Environment. *The Yale Law Journal*, *124*(6): 1934–2024.

Street Sense Media. (September 24, 2019). With Limited Access to Hospital Resources in Wards 7 and 8, local clinics are bridging the gap in Health Care. Retrieved February 14, 2022 from: www.streetsensemedia.org/article/with-limited-access-to-hospital-resources-in-wards-7-and-8-local-clinics-are-bridging-the-gap-in-health-care/#.Ygrjkd_MI2w

Taylor, D. (2014). Toxic Communities, Environmental Racism, Industrial Pollution, and Residential Mobility. New York University Press. ISBN: 9781479852390.

US Department of Education. (2018). Status and Trends in the Education of Racial and Ethnic Groups 2018. National Center for Education Statistics, US Department of Education. Retrieved October 2021 from https://nces.ed.gov/pubs2019/2019038.pdf.

US District Court for District of Columbia. (2011). Consent Decree. Retrieved October 2021 from http://benningservicecenter.com/benning-consent-decree/documents.aspx.

Whittemore, A.H. (2017). The Impact of Racial and Ethnic Minorities with Zoning in the United States. *Journal of Planning Literature*, *32*(1): 16–27.

Yang, I.V., & Schwartz, D.M. (2012). Epigenetic Mechanisms and the Development of Asthma. *The Journal of Allergy and Clinical Immunology*, *130*: 1243–1255.

6

ENVIRONMENTAL JUSTICE AND SMART CITIES

Angela Orebaugh

Smart City Overview

The concept of a smart city may conjure images of the Jetson's with their flying cars, people movers, and automated everything. While we aren't quite there yet, today's smart cities use information and communication technology (ICT) to connect and improve infrastructure, create operational efficiencies, share information, improve the quality of government services, and increase the quality of life, equity, and prosperity of its citizens. Examples of the benefits of smart cities include improved transportation, social services, and sustainability.

Smart cities collect, process, analyze, and share a large amount of data. This data can enhance the quality, performance, and interactivity of urban services; reduce costs and resource consumption; and increase contact between citizens and government. The insights gained from the data are used to manage assets, resources, and services more efficiently, thus improving operations across the city. Smart city data include data collected directly from citizens and remote sensors in buildings and other infrastructure. The data could be used to monitor and manage a variety of community systems including transportation, energy, water, and waste.

The main goal of a smart city is to enhance the quality of life of its citizens through smart technology and informed decision-making. Smart cities give its citizens a voice. This is why smart city strategies start with people, not technology. Smart cities put technology and data to work to make better decisions and deliver a better quality of life. Quality of life has many dimensions including the air that residents breathe, the water they drink, and how safe they feel in the community. Smart cities can use technologies and data to improve some key quality of life indicators by 10–30% (McKinsey, 2018). Quality-of-life improvements include lives saved, reduced health burdens, reduced crime, and clean air and water. A smart

DOI: 10.4324/9781003186076-7

city can take on a number of forms given the diversity of technology and priorities of the city government and inputs from its citizens. Regardless of the form it takes, a smart city should increase civic participation and create sustainable cities with healthy, happy citizens.

Smart Cities Address Civic Problems

Today, 55% of people around the world live in cities. This proportion is expected to increase to 68% by 2050 (Department of Economic and Social Affairs, 2018). Population growth and increased urbanization will add another 2.5 billion people to cities over the next thirty years. With this rapid expansion already straining our cities resources, cities must adapt to the population growth to provide environmental, social, and economic sustainability. In the developing world, the rapid growth of urban area includes more than 1 billion people in overcrowded and polluted slums. In developed countries like the United States, urban areas continue to present a number of challenges for residents and include concentrated pockets of low-income and minority populations that are disproportionately affected by these challenges. To become resilient cities, smart cities must improve energy distribution, streamline waste collection, decrease traffic congestion, and improve air and water quality resulting from increased urbanization. Technologies such as connected traffic lights can reduce traffic congestion by receiving data from sensors and adjusting the timing of traffic lights in response to real-time traffic changes. Smart trash cans send alerts to public services for trash pickup as needed vs. predefined schedules and routes. Smart city sensor technology with wide coverage can identify areas with poor air quality and excessive temperatures. Smart city technology and data can be used to help identify and address inequity issues in urban areas.

Smart Cities Use Data-Driven Approaches

Historically, governments kept data private and shared very little with its citizens. This was due in part to the inability to collect data, data collected in isolated systems, and lack of ability to share data. Smart cities are redefining information sharing through open data. Data is easily collected and shared with smart devices known as the Internet of Things (IoT), a core component of smart cities. The IoT is a vast collection of smart devices that collect, monitor, analyze, and share data from its environment. Smart city IoT devices include sensors to monitor energy distribution and consumption such as smart meters, highway sensors that alert to changing road conditions such as snow and ice, and sensors on city trash cans that alert when they need emptying. The data collected from IoT devices is transmitted and shared using wireless technology and the cloud. Cloud-based applications receive, analyze, and manage data in real time to help cities and its citizens make informed decisions and improve quality of life.

Many smart cities have incorporated open data portals to share the data with its citizens. Open data can facilitate government transparency, accountability, and public participation. Open data also supports technological innovation and economic growth by enabling organizations to develop new kinds of digital applications and services. Smart city open data portals include information such as water consumption data, crime data, public transportation maps and data, bicycling maps and data, community garden and famers market locations, green infrastructure data, tree inventories, sea level rise maps, greenhouse gas emissions, and air quality data (City of New York, n.d.).

Smart Cities Can Support Environmental Justice

The Environmental Protection Agency (EPA) defines environmental justice as the fair treatment and meaningful involvement of all people regardless of race, color, national origin, or income, with respect to the development, implementation, and enforcement of environmental laws, regulations, and policies. This goal will be achieved when everyone enjoys the *same degree of protection from environmental and health hazards, and equal access to the decision-making process to have a healthy environment in which to live, learn, and work.*

Environmental burdens include any environmental pollutant, hazard, or disadvantage that compromises the health or quality of life of residents. Examples include pollution dumping and inadequate access to healthy, affordable food. Smart cities support environmental justice efforts through data collection, sharing, and civic engagement. Smart cities can collect and analyze data to ensure adequate water and energy supplies, proper sanitation services, clean air and water, efficient and affordable public transportation, Internet access, and neighborhood safety and security.

Smart cities facilitate civic engagement and meaningful involvement through a variety of two-way communication opportunities between local government and citizens. Many city agencies maintain an active and responsive presence on social media networks and many of them developed their own citizen apps. The apps can be used to share information and include functionality for citizens to report concerns, collect data, and participate in planning issues. For example, Paris has implemented a participatory budget, inviting anyone to post project ideas and then holding online votes to decide which ones merit funding. Many cities are using third party apps such as MyTown (Realterm Energy, n.d.) and SmartAppCity (n.d.) to enable civic engagement and improve city services. Some cities have developed their own customized app to foster citizen engagement such as the City of Charlottesville's MyCville app (City of Charlottesville, n.d.).

Smart city open data portals also support environmental justice concerns by collecting and sharing data for analysis. Open data can be analyzed to identify problems that need to be addressed. For example, the air quality data may indicate a certain neighborhood is suffering from high levels of toxins, or food accessibility data may indicate food desert areas or lack of access to community gardens or farmers markets for healthy, affordable food.

Smart City Air Quality Monitoring Case Study

The World Health Organization has estimated 91% of the global population lives with pollution above recommended limits and over 4.2 million deaths per year are attributed to outdoor air pollution (World Health Organization, 2021). People living in low- and middle-income countries disproportionately experience the burden of outdoor air pollution with 91% of the 4.2 million deaths occurring in low- and middle-income countries. Smart cities use wireless sensor networks to collect and analyze environmental data such as temperature, humidity, and air quality. Smart technologies can collect highly localized environmental data throughout the city. The air quality data is sent to a cloud-based application for analysis and public viewing. The smart city air quality data can help policymakers identify the areas that need improvements and help citizens to avoid areas that may be especially high on certain days or certain times of the day.

There are many ways smart city technologies can help address outdoor air pollution across a variety of sectors:

- **Industrial:** Smart technologies can help reduce industrial smokestack emissions.
- **Energy:** Smart cities prioritize renewable combustion-free power sources such as solar, wind, or hydropower and the use of low-emission fuels. Smart cities include cogeneration of heat and power and distributed energy generation such as mini-grids and rooftop solar power generation. For consumers, smart cities offer rebates for smart home solutions such as energy efficient appliances, Heating, Ventilation, and Air Conditioning |(HVAC), and lighting.
- **Transportation:** Smart cities prioritize rapid urban transit, walking, and cycling networks as well as rail interurban freight and passenger travel. They include public transportation that uses clean modes of power generation, cleaner heavy-duty diesel vehicles, and low-emission vehicles and fuels.
- **Urban planning:** Smart cities improve the energy efficiency of buildings and make cities greener and more compact, and thus energy efficient.
- **Municipal and agricultural waste management:** Smart cities incorporate strategies for waste reduction, waste separation, recycling and reuse or waste reprocessing. They also include improved methods of biological waste management such as anaerobic waste digestion to produce biogas and low-cost alternatives to the open incineration of solid waste. Smart cities include improved management of urban and agricultural waste, including capture of methane gas emitted from waste sites as an alternative to incineration (for use as biogas).

A case study for air quality monitoring and environmental justice includes a Houston, TX air quality study (Demetillo et al., 2020) performed by several university researchers, NASA, and NOAA. The researchers used satellite data to measure air pollution and found that the levels of nitrogen dioxide (NO_2) were 32% higher in Latino residents, 10% higher for Black residents, and between 15% and 28% higher for residents living below the poverty line. Nitrogen dioxide pollution is linked to higher rates of childhood asthma, increased hospitalizations, and development of cardiovascular diseases. The results can help leaders identify environmental injustices and create policies that specifically target high pollution areas. Although Houston has one of the most robust air quality monitoring sensor networks in the country, only 3% of its residents live within 1.25 miles of an air monitor.

Smart cities need the help of satellite data to fill the gaps between monitors while they are improving their sensor networks. The European Union satellite, Sentinel-5P, carries the TROPOspheric Monitoring Instrument (TROPOMI) which measures environmental quality data such as NO_2. Cities can access this open data for free. As the cost of ground-based sensors decreases, some cities will have sensors on every smart lamppost to provide complete monitoring coverages. Until then cities like Galena Park, part of the Houston metro area, has only one air quality sensor. Galena Park is home to 11,000 residents and is located next to the heavily polluted Houston Ship Channel. Based on data from the study, Galena Park is a hotspot for NO_2 pollution and is also a community of predominantly working-class people of color.

The implementation of widespread air quality monitoring programs can help bridge the gap between the level of exposure to air pollution among communities by identifying areas of higher concentration of pollutants and reducing them through strategies such as including both technologies and policies and regulations.

Smart City Temperature Monitoring Case Study

Cities often experience the urban heat island effect, where areas with little tree cover and high use of materials such as asphalt, concrete, and black roofs absorb the sun's energy and radiate it back out, causing high temperatures than its cooler suburb or rural areas. The Centers for Disease Control and Prevention estimate that more Americans die from heat waves every year than from all other extreme weather events combined. Heat also increases the health impacts of ozone pollution. As climate change causes rising temperatures and cities get hotter, smart cities must find ways to address problem areas (New York City Council, n.d.).

A case study for temperature monitoring in Nature Communications (Hsu et al., 2021) shows that lower income communities and people of color are disproportionately exposed to urban heat island effects and related health issues. The research found that in all but 6 of the 175 largest US cities, people of color have higher heat exposures than white residents. Researchers used satellite temperature readings over the span of four years along with demographic data from the US Census Bureau to compare the temperature in different urban areas. The study showed that the heat island effect temperature was 47% hotter for people of color and low-income residents.

Smart cities collect, analyze, and act upon temperature environmental data, whether ground-based or satellite, to create policies to protect the vulnerable. Areas with higher urban heat island temperatures will benefit from increased tree canopy, green roofs, white reflective roof materials, cool pavement, and cooling centers. Smart cities can use the data to prioritize resources for solutions and address the disparities. For example, the New York City MillionTrees (MillionTreesNYC, n.d.) initiative is preferentially planting trees in six environmental justice neighborhoods that the city's Parks Department identified as neighborhoods with the greatest need for trees. The identified neighborhoods have fewer than average trees and higher than average rates of asthma among young people. The six neighborhoods include Hunts Point, Bronx; Morrisania, Bronx; East New York, Brooklyn; East Harlem, Manhattan; Rockaways, Queens; and Stapleton, Staten Island. The increased tree canopy will help reduce both the heat island effect and air pollution.

Smart City Mobility Case Study

Cities face many mobility challenges that involve both environmental and equity concerns. Smart cities offer high-tech, sustainable solutions, known as smart mobility, that address climate change, advanced social equity and environmental justice, and support economic and community development. Smart mobility can take many forms including public transportation, biking, walking, ride-sharing, car-sharing, and more.

In 2016 Columbus, Ohio won a $40 million Smart City Challenge grant from the US Department of Transportation to demonstrate how modern, integrated transportation options can empower residents to live their best lives (Smart Columbus, 2021). Columbus has implemented a number of technologies under the grant award for safer, cleaner, more equitable transportation options to create opportunity for residents and innovate for the future. Many projects focused on the Linden neighborhood, and opportunity neighborhood with lower income and underserved residents, to show how these technologies can address some of the damage caused by decades of redlining, disinvestment, and isolation caused by interstate construction. The program was built on input and participation from Linden residents and other impacted neighborhoods. Residents worked alongside city staff to show how mobility innovations can be implemented in an equitable way, setting an example for other similar neighborhoods across the United States.

The grant enabled Columbus, Ohio to implement the following eight projects:

- **Connected Electric Autonomous Vehicles:** The Linden LEAP was the nation's first daily-operating public self-driving shuttle in a residential area;

it transported nearly 130,000 meals and 15,000 masks from St. Stephen's Community House to neighbors in need during the pandemic.

- **Prenatal Trip Assistance:** 143 Pregnant individuals with Medicaid coverage participated in Rides4Baby, the prenatal trip assistance research study. Access to on-demand transportation and expanded eligibility criteria for Medicaid-covered rides enabled women access to medical appointments, the pharmacy, and grocery stores or food pantries during their pregnancy and eight weeks postpartum.
- **Multimodal Trip Planning Application:** The Pivot multimodal transportation planning app has been downloaded over 1,000 times supporting 447 trips amidst the pandemic, and can be used as travelers return to downtown.
- **Connected Vehicle Environment:** More than 1,000 vehicles participated in the connected vehicle environment, where vehicles could "talk" to each other and to 85 intersections, 7 of them with the highest crash rates in central Ohio, to understand how the technology can help improve road safety. The technology improved emergency response times and slowed participant speeds in school zones during the demonstration.
- **Event Parking Management:** Federally-funded improvements to the ParkColumbus app make it easier to find and pay for street and garage parking in Downtown and the Short North.
- **Smart Mobility Hubs:** Six smart mobility hubs were constructed in Linden, at Columbus State Community College and at the Easton Transit Center to help fill transportation gaps between bus stops and traveler destinations. The hubs added six interactive kiosks, four scooter charging and bike share stations and one electric vehicle charging station to the neighborhood. The Linden hubs also represented the first expansion of bike share into an opportunity neighborhood.
- **Mobility Assistance for People with Cognitive Disabilities:** In 12 months, 31 individuals with cognitive disabilities used the WayFinder app to take 82 trips independently on public transit, rather than relying on a ride from a caregiver, fostering their independence.
- **Smart Columbus Operating System:** The Smart Columbus Operating System was built largely on open source software that is easy and cost-effective for other cities to implement. The operating system now contains more than 2,000 data sets that have been downloaded more than 220,000 times. The operating system is capable of processing near real-time data, streaming connected vehicle environment data every 15 seconds (Smart Columbus, n.d.).

The Smart Columbus projects demonstrate how an intelligent transportation system and equitable access to transportation can have positive impacts on every day challenges faced by cities. An accessibility analysis found that travelers originating at the Linden Transit Center can now reach at least 20,000 additional jobs and 3,000 additional healthcare services within 30 minutes than using the trip planning tools that existed prior to the introduction of the Smart Columbus projects. Beyond the tangible assets created by the grant, The Ohio State University calculated that investments from the implementation of the USDOT award generated an estimated gross metropolitan product (GMP) of $173.39 million and generated or induced 2,366 jobs (Smart Columbus, n.d.).

Conclusion

Smart cities are resilient cities. They are positioned to address the challenges of increased urban population, climate change, and environmental justice inequities facing today's growing cities. With marginalized communities being disproportionately impacted by environmental issues both historically and in present day, it is important to develop solutions now to work toward a more equitable, sustainable, and resilient future. Smart cities and their associated technologies, open data, and civic participation will pave the way for the future of environmental justice.

Strategies to Help Achieve Resiliency

1. Always include residents in smart city planning and ensure that all voices and communities are heard.
2. Make collected data easily accessed and shared publicly through open data portals.
3. Increase air quality sensor coverage and/or utilize free satellite data such as the TROPOMI.
4. Start early when increasing tree canopy to address the heat island effect as it takes years for trees to mature. When possible plant fast growing trees that also clean the soils such as Poplar.
5. Address mobility challenges for all people including low-income, elderly, youth, pregnant residents, and residents with physical and mental disabilities.
6. Use collected data to prioritize resources for policies, solutions, and disparities.

Discussion/Review Questions

1. What are some hurdles that marginalized communities may face in a developing smart city?
2. What other environmental justice challenges, not discussed in this chapter, can smart cities help address?
3. How can city leaders ensure inclusion so that all residents have a voice in smart city planning?
4. How can smaller cities and towns not located in a large metropolitan area benefit from smart city technologies to address equity concerns?

References

City of Charlottesville. (n.d.). *MyCville app*. Retrieved on September 29, 2021 from www.charlottesville.gov/666/Service-Request.

City of New York. (n.d.). *NYC OpenData*. Retrieved on September 29, 2021 from https://opendata.cityofnewyork.us/

Demetillo, M. A., et al. (2020). *Observing Nitrogen Dioxide Air Pollution Inequality Using High-Spatial-Resolution Remote Sensing Measurements in Houston, TX*. Environmental Science & Technology 54(16), 9882–9895.

Department of Economic and Social Affairs. (2018). *World Urbanization Prospects*. United Nations. https://population.un.org/wup/Publications/Files/WUP2018-KeyFacts.pdf.

Hsu, A., Sheriff, G., Chakraborty, T. et al. (2021). *Disproportionate Exposure to Urban Heat Island Intensity across Major US Cities*. Nature Communications 12, 2721.

McKinsey Global Institute. (2018). *Smart Cities: Digital Solutions for a More Livable Future*. McKinsey & Company. www.mckinsey.com/~/media/mckinsey/business%20functions/operations/our%20insights/smart%20cities%20digital%20solutions%20for%20a%20more%20livable%20future/mgi-smart-cities-full-report.pdf.

MillionTreesNYC. (n.d.). *Getting to a Million Trees, Target Neighborhoods*. Retrieved on September 29, 2021 from www.milliontreesnyc.org/html/about/neighborhoods.shtml.

New York City Council. (n.d.). *Mapping Heath Inequity in NYC*. Retrieved on September 29, 2021 from https://council.nyc.gov/data/heat/

Realterm Energy. (n.d.). *MyTown App*. Retrieved on September 29, 2021 from www.realtermenergy.com/mytown-smart-city/

SmartAppCity. (n.d.). *SmartAppCity*. Retrieved on September 29, 2021 from https://smartappcity.com/en/

Smart Columbus. (n.d.). *U.S. Department of Transportation Grant*. Retrieved on September 29, 2021 from https://smart.columbus.gov/programs/smart-city-demonstration.

Smart Columbus. (2021). *Smart City Challenge Final Report – Executive Summary*. https://d2rfd3nxvhnf29.cloudfront.net/2021-06/20210615-smart-columbus-program-summary-FINAL_0.pdf.

World Health Organization. (2021). *Ambient (Outdoor) Air Pollution*. www.who.int/news-room/fact-sheets/detail/ambient-(outdoor)-air-quality-and-health.

7

ADVANCING ENERGY JUSTICE THROUGH LOCAL CLEAN ENERGY

Seth Mullendore

A California Climate Crisis

Over the past several decades, record temperatures and devastating wildfires have become increasingly commonplace in California. During the five-year period between 2012 and 2016, the state experienced one of the longest and most severe droughts in its history, resulting in billions of dollars in economic losses to agriculture (Lund et al., 2018). Since the 1980s, warmer temperatures and dry conditions exacerbated by climate change have more than doubled the number of days in California with weather conditions during which wildfires are likely to occur (Goss et al., 2020).

Less than 10% of California's wildfires have historically been attributed to electric utility infrastructure, however, power lines have been responsible for around half of the state's most destructive fires (California Public Utilities Commission, 2021b), including the Camp Fire, the deadliest California wildfire to-date. The Camp Fire resulted in the death of 86 people and the destruction of more than 19,000 buildings (Bobrowsky, 2019). In a 2019 order condemning the investor-owned utility found to be responsible for the Camp Fire, Pacific Gas & Electric (PG&E), for a previous violation, Judge William Alsup stated:

> Pacific Gas & Electric company, though the single largest privately-owned utility in America, cannot safely deliver power to California. This failure is upon us because for years, in order to enlarge dividend, bonuses, and political contributions, PG&E cheated on maintenance of its grid – to the point that the grid became unsafe to operate during our annual high winds, so unsafe that the grid itself failed and ignited many catastrophic wildfires.
>
> *United States of America v. Pacific Gas and Electric, 2020*

DOI: 10.4324/9781003186076-8

To minimize the role of electric infrastructure in sparking wildfires, PG&E and the state's other large utilities have begun intentionally shutting off power to millions of Californians during dry, windy weather conditions. The shutoffs often occur with little advance warning and few actions to prepare impacted communities for what could be days without power. The utility-forced outages have endangered the lives and livelihoods of thousands of low-income and historically marginalized community members, creating a new energy justice crisis in California. Before delving further into the climate-induced energy crisis in California, the following sections provide an overview of what is meant by the concept of *energy justice* and an introduction to some of the ways energy justice is being implemented in practice.

Defining Energy Justice

While energy justice has been defined and put into practice in multiple ways (Fuller & McCauley, 2016), each variation begins with the recognition that the current energy system is unjust and includes the same basic tenets at its core. Foundational elements of energy justice include the creation of an energy system that minimizes impacts on communities and ecosystems, ensuring that energy is affordable and accessible to all peoples, and establishing energy decision-making processes that are inclusive of and responsive to the voices and viewpoints of historically marginalized communities. For example, in its Just Energy Policies and Practices Action Toolkit, the National Association for the Advancement of Colored People (NAACP) defines energy justice as "initiatives that provide everyone, regardless of race, gender, etc. with safe, affordable, and sustainable energy" (Franklin et al., 2017). Though the principles of energy justice have been implemented in practice for decades, it was only in the last ten years that the concept began to be more fully recognized and developed within academic circles (Heffron & McCauley, 2017).

The evolution of energy justice as a distinct initiative occurred as a natural outgrowth of social, environmental, and climate movements. Just as access to energy has become pivotal in strategies to reduce poverty, raise standards of living, and improve health, so energy justice has become a key component in advancing social, environmental, and climate justice.

The environmental justice movement connects issues of social justice and civil rights with the recognition of the disproportionate distribution of environmental harms and a call for stronger environmental protections. Climate justice builds upon this framework by elevating the concerns of communities bearing the brunt of extreme weather and rising seas, primarily lower income communities, communities of color, and indigenous populations, that often have fewer economic resources available to respond and adapt to the negative impacts of climate change. Energy justice further expands on the environmental and climate justice movements by elevating the shift away from a fossil-fuel-based energy system as a necessary response to climate change and an opportunity to repair harms unjustly imposed on marginalized communities.

Energy justice is often used interchangeably with the term *energy equity* and is closely related to *energy democracy*. In addition to the principles of sustainability, affordability, and inclusion, energy equity demands that communities disproportionately harmed by the energy industry are centered and prioritized throughout the process of transforming the energy sector into a more just and democratic industry. Impacted communities, often referred to as *frontline communities*, include those populations burdened by the extraction, processing, transportation, and combustion of fossil-fuel resources. Achieving energy equity requires not only that the benefits and harms of the energy system are equally shared among all populations, but also that past injustices are also acknowledged and addressed through targeted remediation to resolve existing inequities (Baker et al., 2019). Such inequities are the result of a long history of racist practices and underinvestment in low-income communities and communities of color.

Energy democracy broadly refers to increased participation in energy system decision-making processes and expanding the ability of communities to influence how energy is produced and consumed. Often, energy democracy is used to describe the equitable development and ownership of distributed energy assets, such as solar photovoltaics (PV). It is also used in the context of shared influence and control over the development of larger energy assets and energy systems, including publicly owned utilities and community energy cooperatives. In nearly all instances, energy democracy initiatives work toward achieving a more equitable distribution of ownership and control of energy resources than the existing system, which is integral to both energy equity and energy justice (Baker et al., 2019).

While energy justice acknowledges the importance of a rapid transition away from fossil fuels to limit the severity of climate change, the energy justice movement is largely guided by the fundamental principle that an energy transition which does not address long-standing injustices, such as environmental racism, economic inequalities, and lack of inclusion in decision-making processes, is not truly transformative and, ultimately, is unsustainable. Climate policy and regulations designed to accelerate the deployment of clean energy resources or reduce greenhouse gas emissions do not necessarily advance energy justice. As stated by the Climate Justice Alliance in their just transition framework (2021), "Transition is inevitable. Justice is not."

Energy Justice in Practice

Affordability

Issues of energy affordability focus on the *energy burdens* faced by individuals and households. Energy burden is a measure of total energy expenses dedicated to pay for electricity, heating, and transportation costs as a proportion of household income. The higher the percentage of energy burden, the higher the percentage of a household's income that is devoted solely to meet energy needs, thus the fewer resources remaining to meet other expenses.

High energy burdens can lead to issues of *energy insecurity*, where households can no longer afford to pay their energy expenses, leading to bill delinquencies, and utility shutoffs. Lack of access to energy can result in devastating impacts on the availability of basic needs, including access to food preparation, clean water, and heating and cooling. A survey conducted by the US Energy Information Administration (EIA) found that, in 2015, 31% of US households reported experiencing difficulties paying energy bills or having the resources to maintain adequate heating and cooling. One in five households had to choose between paying for basic necessities or energy bills, and 14% of households were threatened with an energy service disconnection notice (Energy Information Administration, 2018).

Energy affordability can be addressed in several ways. One method is by reducing the amount of energy needed to perform the same activities, for example through improving building weatherization or the replacement of old appliances with more energy-efficient models. Another method is reducing the price of energy consumed, such as through participation in a community solar program providing electricity at a lower rate than the local electric utility. An example of a program designed to alleviate energy burdens is the Low Income Home Energy Assistance Program (LIHEAP). This program provides federal assistance to help households pay energy bills and improve residences through weatherization and energy-related improvements (US Department of Health & Human Services, 2019). Another program is the District of Columbia's Solar for All initiative to bring solar bill savings to 100,000 low- and moderate-income households (DC Department of Energy and Environment, 2020).

California leads the country in solar installations, with more than one million rooftop solar systems installed at homes and businesses throughout the state. While the vast majority of these systems have been installed in higher income households and neighborhoods, the state has taken steps to increase the adoption of solar PV in lower income communities. To boost solar installations benefiting low-income households, the state launched the Single-Family Affordable Solar Homes (SASH) and the Multifamily Affordable Solar Housing (MASH) programs in 2009. SASH, which is managed by the nonprofit GRID Alternatives, offers a $3 per watt solar incentive for homeowners with a household income of 80% or below the area median income and reside in housing defined as affordable (California Public Utilities Commission, 2021a). The incentive is high enough to cover most, if not all, of the cost of installing a home solar system, however, it is not available to the many Californians that do not own their homes. The MASH program was replaced by the Solar on Multifamily Affordable Housing (SOMAH) program, which launched in 2019 (California Public Utilities Commission, 2021d). SOMAH incentivizes multifamily affordable housing property owners to install solar systems that provide direct economic benefits to residents. The program requires that at least 51% of the energy produced by the system is allocated to reduce tenant electric bills and offers higher incentive levels for the portion of the solar system designated to serve residents.

Access

Lack of access to energy is also known as *energy poverty*. While energy poverty is commonly thought of as only a concern for less-developed countries, many families face energy poverty in developed economies as well. In 2000, the EIA reported that 14.2% of Native American households living on reservations suffered from lack of access to electricity, compared to the national average of 1.4% (Energy Information Administration, 2000).

In remote locations where connection to the electric grid is challenging, energy poverty is beginning to be addressed through the development of small, self-contained power systems, called *microgrids*. Microgrids are able to deliver power independently of the central power system, whether connected to the utility grid or completely off-grid. They can be powered by a combination of resources, most commonly solar PV, energy storage, combined heat and power (CHP), and conventional diesel and natural gas generators. Microgrids primarily powered by solar PV paired with battery storage have become increasingly common in many regions, particularly those with plentiful solar resources. The US Trade and Development Agency is funding an effort to develop up to 134 solar microgrids to deliver power to 100,000 households in Cameroon (US Trade and Development Agency, 2021), where nearly 40% of the population lacked access to electricity as recently as 2018 (World Bank, 2018).

In 2021, PG&E submitted a proposal to the California Public Utilities Commission (CPUC) to replace power lines serving a small number of customers in remote locations with microgrids. The utility determined that developing microgrids with solar, battery storage, and generators would be more cost-effective than the long-term expense of maintaining power lines stretching across difficult terrain in wildfire-prone areas. PG&E identified several hundred sites that could be economically viable candidates for solar PV and battery storage to replace traditional utility infrastructure (St. John, 2021).

Impacts

In addressing the distribution of impacts resulting from the energy sector, many factors must be considered, including environmental, health, and economic impacts. The negative impacts of energy production, distribution, and consumption—environmental degradation, air pollution, climate change—are key components of the environmental justice and climate justice movements, in addition to energy justice. Equitable distribution of these harms requires more than just an equal sharing of negative effects across all populations consuming an energy resource.

Historically disproportionate harms must also be addressed through fair compensation to remediate past ecological damages and adverse public health conditions already impacting communities, a form of restorative justice (Salter et al., 2018). Along with negative impacts, there are positive factors to consider, such as job opportunities, wealth creation, and energy resilience. Equitable participation in the energy workforce and in the ownership of energy assets can help to lift economically marginalized communities. Access to reliable, resilient sources of energy during times of crisis can help communities respond to and recover from extreme events, like severe weather.

Achieving a truly equitable allocation of energy-related harms and benefits, distributive justice, is no small task. One example of efforts to rebalance the negative impacts of fossil-fuel power generation on low-income communities of color is an initiative in New York City to accelerate the retirement of much of the city's fleet of urban power plants and replace the assets with renewable generation and energy storage (PEAK Coalition & Strategen Consulting, 2021). The initiative is being led by a coalition of environmental advocates and community-based organizations, including two communities burdened by multiple power plants, Sunset Park and Hunts Point. The coalition is calling for significant investments in local clean energy development and community-owned energy resources. One of the organizations involved in the effort, UPROSE, organized the successful development of New York City's first cooperatively owned community solar project, a 685-kilowatt rooftop solar development called Sunset Park Solar. The solar project is empowering the Sunset Park neighborhood through local ownership, local job training, and electricity bill savings for residents and businesses (UPROSE, 2020).

The New York City initiative was inspired by emerging community-led battles to stop power plants in other locations, primarily California. The most notable of these was a community movement against a proposed gas power plant in Oxnard, California. Activists from Oxnard's working-class immigrant community organized a campaign that succeeded in reversing the approval of a 262-megawatt gas power plant, the Puente Power Plant (Central Coast Alliance United for a Sustainable Economy, 2021). As an alternative to the power plant, the utility serving Oxnard, Southern California Edison, selected a diverse portfolio of battery storage projects that will be distributed throughout the region.

Participation

Energy justice cannot be achieved without transparent, equitable, and inclusive decision-making processes. This requires transparent processes that engage and include voices representative of all potentially impacted communities in fair and meaningful ways—procedural justice. Additionally, the viewpoints of all participants must be treated with respect regardless of economic standing, race, ethnicity, gender identity, or any other characteristic—recognition justice (Salter et al., 2018). Through energy justice, the concerns of frontline communities and historically marginalized populations are not merely considered in the steward-ship of energy systems but centered and prioritized throughout energy planning and management processes. A shift toward more inclusive participation and more equitable distribution of power in energy decision-making enables communities to shape and influence the energy transformation to reflect the collective goals and values of their residents. This shift toward energy democracy is key in ensuring a just and responsibly managed energy system and advancing the development of community-based solutions to resolve issues of energy affordability, energy access, and distribution of energy impacts.

In California, the rise of Community Choice Aggregators (CCAs) as an alter-native to traditional utilities has created a potential pathway to expand community participation in energy decisions. CCAs are nonprofit energy providers formed by city and county governments and governed by boards of elected officials. They were established to give communities more direct control over the sources of power delivered to community members, often with the intent of pursuing spe-cific objectives such as reducing the cost of energy for customers, procuring higher levels of renewable energy generation, securing locally sourced energy generation, and, increasingly, advancing social benefits like local workforce development and energy resilience for vulnerable populations. More than 11 million customers are now served by CCAs in California.

However, there is no guarantee that a proliferation of CCAs will lead to equit-able participation in energy processes. To help create a framework for fostering greater energy democracy and energy justice within the CCA structure, the California Environmental Justice Alliance published a set of guiding principles for CCAs to improve engagement with community members, including coordination with local community-based organizations, providing accessible information, pur-suing meaningful outreach efforts, creating opportunities for the community-driven design of programs, and establishing transparent decision-making processes (Behles et al., 2020).

Public Safety Power Shutoffs: A California Energy Crisis

In 2012, the CPUC ruled that the state's electric utilities have the authority to shutoff parts of the power system to prevent utility infrastructure from causing or contributing to fires during certain weather conditions, such as strong winds and hot, dry weather. These shutoff events, or de-energizations, are officially called Public Safety Power Shutoffs (PSPS). The temporary shutoff events can cut off power to millions of customers at a time and, in many cases, last for multiple days.

During PSPS events that occurred in October 2019, more than one million PG&E customers had their power shutoff, leaving nearly three million residents without access to electricity. Many households had little to no warning prior to losing power, leaving them completely unprepared (Newburger, 2019). For lower income households, loss of electricity can result in many hardships, including loss of food, loss of income due to missed work, and dangerous living conditions due to lack of heating and cooling and lack of access to clean water (Wong-Parodi, 2020). For individuals with electricity-dependent medical needs, an unexpected outage can be a life-threatening event. After cutting off power to 729,000 customers during one four-day period, PG&E admitted that it had failed to alert 23,000 customers, including 500 customers with critical medical needs (Serna, 2019).

Local Clean Energy: An Energy Justice Strategy

The clean energy transition, the move away from polluting fossil-fuel generation toward an energy system primarily powered by wind, water, and solar, offers a unique opportunity to advance energy justice. This is particularly true of local, distributed clean energy resources, in particular solar PV and battery storage, which can be installed almost anywhere and at almost any scale. Along with the obvious climate benefits of reducing reliance on greenhouse gas-emitting fossil-fuel power plants, greater adoption of solar PV and battery storage can open avenues to improve public health, strengthen community resilience, reduce energy burdens, alleviate energy poverty, build wealth, and advance energy democracy.

Climate and Public Health

When a solar system generates electricity, it does not produce any emissions. By offsetting the need for fossil-fuel generation, solar energy reduces the release of climate-damaging greenhouse gases, such as carbon dioxide and methane. However, one downside of solar generation is that it is an intermittent resource, meaning that it can't be turned on and off or up and down like traditional sources of power generation. When the sun is shining, solar is producing. That doesn't always match up with how energy is being consumed.

Adding energy storage to solar changes this. By incorporating battery storage, the output from a solar system can be regulated by storing a portion of the energy to be discharged at a later time, making solar energy a more flexible and responsive resource. With battery storage, stored solar energy can be consumed at any time, whether the sun is out or not. It can make solar more effective at reducing harmful emissions by releasing clean energy onto the grid when the most polluting resources would otherwise be operating. Even small systems can have a big impact. Some projects, called virtual power plants, aggregate hundreds, in some cases thousands, of small, distributed solar and battery storage systems to collectively displace the need for large power plants (Mullendore, 2019).

Reducing the utilization of coal and gas for power generation also means fewer local emissions, such as nitrogen oxides and fine particulates. Long-term exposure to both the pollutants can result in severe public health impacts. Like with greenhouse gas emissions, electricity produced by a solar system and stored in batteries can be used to specifically target periods when local air emissions are high, often during times of high system-wide demand for energy, called peak demand. Peak demand is typically met by expensive to run, inefficient power plants known as peakers that are often located near population centers and can be significant contributors to local air pollution (PEAK Coalition & Strategen Consulting, 2020). Battery storage paired with renewable generation can serve as a cost-effective and emission-free alternative to these polluting power plants (PEAK Coalition & Strategen Consulting, 2021).

Of course, no technology is without its downsides. Both solar panels and battery cells are composed of raw materials that must be mined and processed, which can result in climate, environmental, and social impacts. The full life-cycle impact, from extraction to end-of-life, must also be considered when assessing the relative benefits of various energy technologies.

Energy Resilience

It is not by chance that communities of color and lower income neighborhoods are disproportionately impacted by climate-induced disasters and power outages. A long history of systemic racism forced many Black, Indigenous, and People of Color (BIPOC) communities to relocate and settle on marginal pieces of land. Lack of adequate investment in infrastructure, supportive institutions, and planning has left these communities vulnerable to extreme weather events, whether in the form of wildfires, heat waves, flooding, ice storms, tornadoes, derechos, or hurricanes.

Energy resilience is closely intertwined with health. Without access to energy, many basic services can become severely limited or completely unavailable during emergencies, including clean water, food preparation and refrigeration, and temperature regulation. This lack of access can lead to significant health impacts, as occurred in Puerto Rico after Hurricane Maria decimated the island's electric grid and left residents without power for months (Kishore et al., 2018).

When solar PV and battery storage are configured to deliver backup power during grid outages, they can directly improve health outcomes for individuals and communities during times of crisis (Mango & Shapiro, 2019). This is particularly critical for households dependent on electricity to power medical devices. In the United States, more than 2.5 million people rely on electricity to power home medical equipment (US Department of Health & Human Services, 2021). Based on a national survey of older adults with electricity-dependent medical needs, only about 25% of respondents were prepared for power outages with an alternate source of power (Bell et al., 2020). With 185,000 electricity-dependent Medicare beneficiaries, California has the highest population of medically vulnerable individuals of any state.

In addition to households, solar PV paired with battery storage can power community facilities providing essential services, such as food banks, emergency shelters, health clinics, and first responders. Access to the services provided by these types of facilities can be critical to avoiding serious, in many cases life-threatening, health outcomes during major disruptions, particularly for frontline communities already suffering from deep health, environmental, and economic inequities.

Energy Insecurity and Building Wealth

As previously discussed, solar PV and battery storage can help to address energy poverty through the development of microgrids providing access to energy in remote regions that are difficult to serve through traditional utility infrastructure. By reducing the cost of electric bills, the technologies can also act to alleviate energy insecurity and energy poverty resulting from utility disconnections due to delinquency. According to a study evaluating utility shutoffs from ten states that require disclosure of customer disconnects, more than 760,000 households lost their access to electricity during the one-year period marked by the start of the COVID pandemic crisis in the United States (Greer, 2021). Lowering the cost of energy bills for these households may have helped avoid many of these disconnections.

Solar PV can be a powerful tool to reduce high energy burdens. It is the only source of clean electricity generation that can be installed almost anywhere, and, once installed, a solar system can continue producing power for 30 years or more. For households and businesses that are not able to directly install solar on their property, whether due to lack of suitable space, ownership issues, or other challenges, many states have developed community solar programs allowing customers to purchase a share of a collectively owned solar system. Due to challenges in how community solar has been implemented in the state, California has experienced little uptake of community solar as compared to other leading states.

In some cases, battery storage can enable greater electric bill savings than solar alone. For customers on time-of-use electric rate tariffs, where electricity costs are highest during peak pricing periods, batteries can store solar energy during times of low electricity prices and discharge to during peak periods to offset higher priced electricity, resulting in increased overall savings. Many commercial customers are on electric utility tariffs with demand-related charges, which are based on the rate of electricity consumption, measured in kilowatts. Batteries can discharge to target periods of high onsite demand to reduce these charges, a process called *peak shaving* (Clean Energy Group & National Renewable Energy Laboratory, 2017).

In addition to electric bill reductions, batteries can create opportunities for wealth creation. Some states, utilities, and regional transmission operators offer programs that compensate battery system owners for services provided to the grid. These services include operating the battery system to balance fluctuations in the frequency and voltage of the electric grid and discharging in response to utility signals during times of high system-wide electricity demand. One such program is ConnectedSolutions in Massachusetts, which compensates battery storage system owners up to $250 per kilowatt each year that the system participates in the program (Mullendore et al., 2021). A typical residential battery system could earn around $1,000 per year through participation in ConnectedSolutions.

Energy Democracy

There are long-standing examples of public participation in the energy system, most notably community-owned electric cooperatives, publicly owned utilities, and, more recently, CCAs. However, the leadership of these institutions is often not representative of the communities served and community members rarely see direct economic benefits as a result of limited opportunities to participate in the energy decision-making process. While the vast majority of electric utilities are cooperatives or publicly owned entities, more than 70% of customers in the United States get their electricity from private, investor-owned utilities (Darling & Hoff, 2019). Historically, individuals and communities have been largely removed from the energy decision-making process.

Distributed renewable energy has upended the traditional, top-down utility model of large, centralized power plants supplying electricity in a one-way flow to customers. With solar PV, customers have the ability to take ownership over how the energy they consume is produced. The inclusion of battery storage takes this step further, allowing customers to control when the energy produced by their solar system is consumed, stored for later use, or exported to the grid and distributed to other customers. Few communities have attempted to collectively purchase a large power plant, but community ownership of solar is increasingly common. The development of community-based solar PV and battery storage installations also create opportunities for more diverse participation in the clean energy economy through the implementation of local hiring and workforce development requirements and prioritizing the engagement of locally owned business for project engineering and construction.

Unfortunately, there are still many barriers to solar and battery storage ownership among low-income populations and communities of color. The highest rates of solar adoption are found among higher income households in neighborhoods with relatively low Black and Latinx populations (Barbose et al., 2021). Researchers have found racial disparities in solar PV installations even when accounting for differences in income and home ownership. Black communities have been found to have solar adoption rates that are 60% lower than communities with no racial majority (Sunter et al., 2019). Latinx communities have installation rates of 30% less than those with no racial majority when accounting for income and 45% less when home ownership is considered.

Cost remains the most significant barrier to the broader uptake of solar PV and battery storage. Despite dramatic cost declines in both technologies over the last decade, solar PV and battery storage installations still require significant upfront investments. The federal investment tax credit (ITC) has been a driving factor in accelerating the uptake of solar; however, the tax incentives cannot be directly realized by nonprofit entities or individuals with no tax liability. Third-party ownership options are available to help overcome these barriers, but they result in less benefit reaching the customer and do little to advance energy democracy.

Energy Justice and California's Self-Generation Incentive Program

Despite the potential of solar PV and battery storage to further many aspects of energy justice, the technologies alone will not necessarily result in any significant movement toward greater equity and inclusion in the energy sector. Solar PV and battery storage are tools that can be used to help achieve the goals of energy justice but not solutions in and of themselves. Without policies and programs in place to ensure the equitable deployment of technologies like solar and battery storage, the clean energy transition may keep advancing while leaving the same inequities in place.

In addition to its low-income solar programs, California is one of the few states with a dedicated energy storage incentive. The state's Self-Generation Incentive Program (SGIP) began as a distributed generation incentive when it was first authorized in 2001, mainly targeting customer-sited solar (California Public Utilities Commission, 2021c). Over time, solar was phased out of the program, and SGIP evolved to focus on incentivizing energy storage. SGIP provides rebates for battery systems at homes and businesses, with the goal of reducing greenhouse gas emissions. The program ran for more than a decade before incorporating any form of energy justice considerations.

In 2017, the CPUC established an Equity budget within SGIP in recognition of the fact that the program was not catalyzing battery storage development in California's most underserved communities. The CPUC allocated 25% of SGIP funds to the Equity budget for projects located in low-income communities and state-designated disadvantaged communities, which are determined based on a number of social and environmental justice considerations. However, a mix of factors left those funds underutilized. Incentives for the Equity budget were initially set at the same level as the rest of SGIP funds, which had already failed to produce an equitable distribution of projects. The low incentive levels, combined with poor outreach and education and incongruities with potentially complimentary programs like SASH, resulted in a failure to produce projects in the communities the Equity budget was meant to serve (Mullendore & Milford, 2019). More than a year after becoming available, the $72 million Equity budget had not been allocated to support a single battery storage project.

SGIP underwent another transformation in 2020, when California regulators authorized an additional $1 billion for the program and created an Equity Resiliency budget in response to the widespread wildfire-related utility shutoffs of 2019. The Equity Resiliency budget designated $600 million in funds to essentially offset the entire installed cost of a battery storage system designed to provide backup power for households and community services providers in low-income and disadvantaged communities located in high wildfire-threat zones or that had experienced multiple PSPS events. Households with critical medical needs are also eligible for the Equity Resiliency incentives. At the same time, the CPUC raised the level of Equity budget incentives to $850 per kilowatt-hour, not as high as the Equity Resiliency budget but high enough to cover the majority of the cost of a battery storage system.

Unfortunately, the rollout of the new version of SGIP also had its issues. Applications opened for the new Equity Resiliency budget and higher Equity budget incentives in May 2020. By early July, before utility-designed community outreach plans were even finalized, the majority of the funds were already allocated to projects, including all of the Equity and Equity Resiliency incentives available to PG&E customers. Additionally, controversies surfaced that a significant portion of Equity Resiliency budget funds were being allocated to support battery systems at the second homes of wealthier Californians instead of low-income and medically vulnerable residents threatened by wildfire-related power outages (Sangree, 2020).

RYSE Center: Implementing Energy Justice in Richmond, CA

RYSE Center opened in 2008 to create a safe space for the youth of Richmond, California to "love, learn, educate, heal, and transform lives and communities" (RYSE, 2021). Located in one of California's most environmentally impacted neighborhoods, RYSE is a youth-led community center providing programs and organizing events for young members of the community, from ages 13 to 21. Richmond is home to multiple serious environmental justice hazards, including port activities, major highways, and the Chevron oil refinery, which is one of the state's largest sources of greenhouse gas emissions. About 80% of Richmond residents are working-class people of color. Nearly 15% of the population lives on incomes below the poverty line.

RYSE is collaborating with the Asian Pacific Environmental Network (APEN), a member-based, grassroots environmental justice organization based in Oakland and Richmond, to develop a community-owned, resilient solar PV, and battery storage system at RYSE Center (Lou et al., 2020). The project is part of a larger development that will expand the existing facility threefold with the construction of a new space called RYSE Commons. APEN is helping to coordinate the design process through a youth-driven approach that centers on the concerns, interests, and needs of the community served by RYSE through a series of facilitated conversations. The solar PV system paired with battery storage will deliver energy cost savings to RYSE and provide a foundation of energy resilience for the facilities, but the goals of the initiative go beyond energy alone.

RYSE and APEN are working with a youth advisory group to transform the RYSE Center facilities into a fully functional Resilience Hub designed to meet everyday community needs and strengthen community resilience before, during, and after emergencies (Lou et al., 2020). In this context, a Resilience Hub represents an existing trusted local resource that provides services to the surrounding community, serving as a place of community gathering, sharing, and organizing and a point of access for social services. During extreme weather and other disruptive events, a Resilience Hub can be mobilized to support community response and recovery services (Baja et al., 2019). Energy resilience provided by onsite generation and energy storage, though critical during power outages, is just one of many essential components that may be incorporated as part of a community Resilience Hub.

The RYSE project has successfully secured funding support and technical assistance through partnerships with mission-aligned nonprofit organizations. Through a series of interactive workshops, the youth advisory group is in the process of identifying and prioritizing the concerns and needs of RYSE community members during a variety of emergency scenarios to determine the backup power needs a solar PV and battery storage system should be designed to meet. Energy savings and any revenue generated from the systems are planned to be pooled into a youth-directed fund.

As with many community projects, the transformation of the RYSE Center into a Resilience Hub has been impacted and delayed by COVID-19. Installation of the solar system was expected to begin before the end of 2021. RYSE Center is on a waitlist for SGIP incentives to support the battery portion of the system. When completed, the RYSE Center Resilience Hub will serve as a community-first model for advancing energy justice in communities across California and beyond.

Energy Justice in an Age of Uncertainty

California is far from alone in confronting unprecedented weather conditions. Each year brings a new reminder of the climate crisis facing humanity and the importance of reliable access to energy, whether in the form of extreme heat in the Pacific Northwest, extreme cold in the Southwest, or powerful storms impacting communities along the Gulf and East Coast. While such extreme events can have devastating impacts, it is often during the power outages that frequently follow when death tolls rise as essential services become unavailable and vulnerable populations struggle to survive. Each event reaffirms that access to energy must be treated as a basic human right.

The world is in the midst of a massive energy transition. In the absence of energy justice, that transition will miss the opportunity to be truly transformational. Applying the principles of energy justice – minimizing harm, ensuring access and affordability, establishing inclusive processes – can lead to a new energy system where people are able to reclaim sovereignty over how energy is produced and consumed, an energy system powered by clean, sustainable resources, a resilient and just energy system that benefits and uplifts all communities.

Discussion/Review Questions

1. What is energy justice? How does energy justice relate to similar initiatives, such as environmental justice and climate justice?
2. In what ways have PSPS events impacted energy justice in California? What are some measures that California has implemented to address energy justice issues?
3. How has RYSE incorporated energy justice into its Resilience Hub initiative? What additional strategies could communities take to engage members in advancing energy justice?

References

Baja, K., McKinstry-Wu, S., Oxnam, G., & Fitzgerald, G. (2019). *Guide to Developing Resilience Hubs* (Rep.). Retrieved from http://resilience-hub.org/wp-content/uploads/2019/10/USDN_ResilienceHubsGuidance-1.pdf

Baker, S., DeVar, S., & Prakash, S. (2019). *The Energy Justice Workbook* (Rep.). Retrieved from https://iejusa.org/wp-content/uploads/2019/12/The-Energy-Justice-Workbook-2019-web.pdf

Barbose, G. L., Forrester, S., O'Shaughnessy, E., & Darghouth, N. R. (2021, April). *Residential Solar-Adopter Income and Demographic Trends: 2021 Update* (Rep.). Retrieved from https://eta-publications.lbl.gov/sites/default/files/solar-adopter_income_trends_final.pdf

Behles, D., Sutterman, A., Torres, J., Raval, A., Diaz, A., Portillo, E., ... Lazerow, S. (2020). *Building a Just Energy Future: A Framework for Community Choice Aggregators to Power Equity and Democracy in California* (Rep.). Retrieved from https://caleja.org/wp-content/uploads/2020/11/CEJA-CCA-REPORT-FINAL-SINGLE-PAGE.pdf

Bell, S. A., Iwashyna, J., Kirch, M., Kullgren, J., Malani, P., Singer, D., & Solway, E. (2020, February). After the Storm: The Health Impacts of Weather and Climate-Related Disasters on Older Adults in the U.S. Retrieved from https://ihpi.umich.edu/news/ihpi-briefs/disasters

Bobrowsky, M. (2019, August 8). Camp Fire Death Toll Rises to 86 after Man Who Suffered Third-Degree Burns Dies. Retrieved from www.sacbee.com/news/california/fires/article233683422.html

California Public Utilities Commission. (2021a). CSI Single-Family Affordable Solar Homes (SASH) Program. Retrieved April 26, 2021, from www.cpuc.ca.gov/General.aspx?id=3043

California Public Utilities Commission. (2021b). Public Safety Power Shutoff (PSPS)/De-Energization. Retrieved April 24, 2021, from www.cpuc.ca.gov/deenergization/

California Public Utilities Commission. (2021c). Self-Generation Incentive Program. Retrieved April 26, 2021, from www.cpuc.ca.gov/sgip/

California Public Utilities Commission. (2021d). Solar on Multifamily Affordable Housing. Retrieved April 26, 2021, from https://calsomah.org/

Central Coast Alliance United for a Sustainable Economy. (2021). Defeating the Puente Power Plant. Retrieved from https://causenow.org/our-work/defeating-puente-power-plant

Clean Energy Group & National Renewable Energy Laboratory. (2017). *An Introduction to Demand Charges* (Rep.). Retrieved from www.cleanegroup.org/wp-content/uploads/Demand-Charge-Fact-Sheet.pdf

Climate Justice Alliance. (2021, February 19). Just Transition. Retrieved April 6, 2021, from https://climatejusticealliance.org/just-transition

Darling, D., & Hoff, S. (2019, August 15). Investor-Owned Utilities Served 72% of U.S. Electricity Customers in 2017. Retrieved from www.eia.gov/todayinenergy/detail. php?id=40913#

DC Department of Energy and Environment. (2020). Solar for All. Retrieved April 8, 2021, from https://doee.dc.gov/solarforall

Energy Information Administration. (2000). *Energy Consumption and Renewable Energy Development Potential on Indian Lands* (Rep.). Retrieved from www.energy.gov/sites/ prod/files/2017/06/f34/EIA2000.pdf

Energy Information Administration. (2018, September 19). One in Three U.S. Households Faces a Challenge in Meeting Energy Needs. Retrieved from www.eia.gov/ todayinenergy/detail.php?id=37072

Franklin, M., Taylor, K., Steichen, L., Saseedhar, S., Kennedy, E., Alksnis, M., … Patterson, J. (2017). *Just Energy Policies and Practices Action Toolkit: Glossary* (Rep.). Retrieved from www.naacp.org/wp-content/uploads/2014/03/Glossary_JEP-Action-Toolkit_ NAACP.pdf

Fuller, S., & McCauley, D. (2016). Framing Energy Justice: Perspectives from Activism and Advocacy. *Energy Research & Social Science, 11*, 1–8. doi:10.1016/j.erss.2015.08.004

Goss, M., Swain, D. L., Abatzoglou, J. T., Sarhadi, A., Kolden, C. A., Williams, A. P., & Diffenbaugh, N. S. (2020). Climate Change Is Increasing the Likelihood of Extreme Autumn Wildfire Conditions across California. *Environmental Research Letters, 15*(9). doi:10.1088/1748-9326/ab83a7

Greer, R. (2021). *Power Crisis: Despite Transparency Failures, Utility Information Reveals Major Home Shutoff Problem More Than 765,000 Household Power Disconnects Reported Across 10 States* (Rep.). Retrieved from www.biologicaldiversity.org/programs/energy-justice/ pdfs/Power-Crisis-Report-March-2021.pdf

Heffron, R. J., & McCauley, D. (2017). The Concept of Energy Justice across the Disciplines. *Energy Policy, 105*, 658–667. doi:10.1016/j.enpol.2017.03.018

Kishore, N., Marqués, D., Mahmud, A., Kiang, M.V., Rodriguez, I., Fuller, A., … Buckee, C. O. (2018). Mortality in Puerto Rico after Hurricane Maria. *New England Journal of Medicine, 379*(2), 162–170. doi:10.1056/nejmsa1803972

Lou, Z., Raval, A., Young, M., & Appel, S. (2020). *Resilience before Disaster: The Need to Build Equitable, Community-Driven Social Infrastructure* (Rep.). Retrieved from http://apen4ej. org/wp-content/uploads/2020/10/Resilience-Before-Disaster-FINAL-UPDATED.pdf

Lund, J., Medellin-Azuara, J., Durand, J., & Stone, K. (2018). Lessons from California's 2012– 2016 Drought. *Journal of Water Resources Planning and Management, 144*(10), 04018067. doi:10.1061/(asce)wr.1943-5452.0000984

Mango, M., & Shapiro, A. (2019, June 4). *Home Health Care in the Dark: Why Climate, Wildfires and Other Risks Call for New Resilient Energy Storage Solutions to Protect Medically Vulnerable Households From Power Outages* (Rep.). Retrieved from www.cleangroup. org/wp-content/uploads/Home-Health-Care-in-the-Dark.pdf

Mullendore, S. (2019, June 24). Small Solar and Battery Storage Systems Are Toppling Power Plants. Retrieved from www.cleangroup.org/small-solar-and-battery-storage- systems-are-toppling-power-plants/

Mullendore, S., & Milford, L. (2019, September 4). California Aims to Fix Low-Income Storage Program and Deliver New Resilience Incentives. Retrieved from www. cleangroup.org/california-aims-to-fix-low-income-storage-program-and-deliver- new-resilience-incentives/

Mullendore, S., Olinsky-Paul, T., Oxnam, G., Simpkins, T., & Simpkins, A. (2021). *Connected Solutions: The New Economics of Solar+Storage for Affordable Housing in Massachusetts* (Rep.). Retrieved from www.cleanegroup.org/wp-content/uploads/connected-solutions-affordable-housing.pdf

Newburger, E. (2019, October 27). More Than 2 Million People Expected to Lose Power in PG&E Blackout as California Wildfires Rage. Retrieved from www.cnbc.com/2019/10/26/pge-will-shut-off-power-to-940000-customers-in-northern-california-to-reduce-wildfire-risk.html

PEAK Coalition & Strategen Consulting. (2020, May 7). *Dirty Energy, Big Money: How Private Companies Make Billions from Polluting Fossil Fuel Peaker Power Plants in New York City's Environmental Justice Communities – and How to Create a Cleaner, More Just Alternative* (Rep.). Retrieved from www.cleanegroup.org/wp-content/uploads/Dirty-Energy-Big-Money.pdf

PEAK Coalition & Strategen Consulting. (2021, March 16). *The Fossil Fuel End Game: A Frontline Vision to Retire New York City's Peaker Plants by 2030* (Rep.). Retrieved from www.cleanegroup.org/wp-content/uploads/Fossil-Fuel-End-Game.pdf

RYSE. (2021). RYSE Center. Retrieved April 27, 2021, from https://rysecenter.org/

Salter, R., Gonzalez, C. G., & Kronk Warner, E. A. (2018). Energy Justice: Frameworks for Energy Law and Policy. In *Energy Justice: US and International Perspectives* (pp. 4–14). Cheltenham: Edward Elgar Publishing. doi:10.4337/9781786431769

Sangree, H. (2020, October 12). PSPS Relief Funds Not Spent as Intended, CPUC Says. Retrieved from https://rtoinsider.com/rto/psps-relief-funds-not-spent-as-intended-cpuc-175609/

Serna, J. (2019, October 28). PG&E Failed to Notify 23,000 of Blackouts; CPUC Launches Probe of Utility Power Outages. Retrieved from www.latimes.com/story/2019-10-28/pge-admits-equipment-failures-power-outages-kincade-fire

St. John, J. (2021, February 2). PG&E Plans Utility-Owned 'Remote Grids' for Isolated Communities. Retrieved from www.greentechmedia.com/articles/read/pge-plans-utility-owned-remote-grids-for-isolated-communities

Sunter, D. A., Castellanos, S., & Kammen, D. M. (2019). Disparities in Rooftop Photovoltaics Deployment in the United States by Race and Ethnicity. *Nature Sustainability, 2*(1), 71–76. doi:10.1038/s41893-018-0204-z

United States of America v. Pacific Gas and Electric (United States District Court Northern District of California) (2020, April 29). Retrieved from https:// assets.documentcloud.org/documents/6880045/Alsup-Pge-200429.pdf

UPROSE. (2020). Sunset Park Solar. Retrieved from www.uprose.org/sunset-park-solar

US Department of Health & Human Services. (2019, November 1). Low Income Home Energy Assistance Program (LIHEAP). Retrieved from www.acf.hhs.gov/ocs/low-income-home-energy-assistance-program-liheap

US Department of Health & Human Services. (2021, February 5). HHS emPOWER Map. Retrieved April 20, 2021, from https://empowermap.hhs.gov/

US Trade and Development Agency. (2021, March 25). *USTDA Supports Clean Energy Access in Cameroon* [Press release]. Retrieved from https://ustda.gov/ustda-supports-clean-energy-access-in-cameroon/

Wong-Parodi, G. (2020). When Climate Change Adaptation Becomes a "Looming Threat" to Society: Exploring Views and Responses to California Wildfires and Public Safety Power Shutoffs. *Energy Research & Social Science, 70.* doi:10.1016/j.erss.2020.101757

World Bank. (2018). Access to Electricity (% of Population). Retrieved April 10, 2021, from https://data.worldbank.org/indicator/EG.ELC.ACCS.ZS

8

EMERGENCY MANAGEMENT AND ENVIRONMENTAL JUSTICE

Disaster Preparedness in Vulnerable Communities

Jim Redick

Introduction

You knocked this one out of the park! Those are your thoughts as you conclude a civic league presentation on the importance of having flood insurance. Having covered all the main points, those in attendance now understand a property does not need to reside in a flood zone to experience flooding and flood insurance is likely not part of their homeowner's or renter's policy. They are also fully aware of the advantages flood insurance has in the speed of recovery versus post-disaster loans that must be repaid, and if they do not act soon, they will not have coverage when hurricane season begins in just a month away. To help emphasize your point, you came prepared with the most up-to-date colorful maps reflecting all the Repetitive Loss and Severe Repetitive Loss properties in your coastal community—over one thousand properties in all! And, further, impressed everyone by handing out copies of Federal Emergency Management Agency's (FEMA) Estimated Flood Loss Potential chart that calculates the potential financial losses per inch of flooding. Of course, after discussing the threat you also promoted opportunities to minimize or eliminate future impacts of flooding through FEMA's Hazard Mitigation Assistance (HMA) program. During the group's obligatory applause, you think with all the information presented, who would possibly choose not to get coverage or consider mitigating their vulnerable property? Your thoughts are validated by the list of individuals interested in follow up conversations. Successful evening? Sure! On the face of it folks who attended left with more important knowledge than when they came. However, if this is the extent of your outreach, you may not be meeting the needs of all in your community and may also fall short of legal requirements.

DOI: 10.4324/9781003186076-9

Emergency management can be described as the discipline responsible for the overall preparedness and resilience of a community. With an understanding of the natural and man-made threats to which a community could be vulnerable, the emergency manager works to take steps necessary to minimize or eliminate these threats, to prepare for that which is inevitable, lead the response efforts and then navigate the recovery toward a stronger future. To say it is a crucial position is an understatement and there are many skills necessary to be successful. First, it is important to identify exactly who tends to fill these crucial positions. The US Department of Labor shows at least five years' experience and a college degree are the norm for an Emergency Management Director (US Bureau of Labor Statistics). DATAUSA shows the overwhelming majority of emergency management directors at 71% are White (non-Hispanic) with the next most common race being Black (non-Hispanic) at 11.7%. Males are the majority at 65.2% and the average salary in the year 2021 is $80,680 (Data USA)—hardly the makeup of most communities. Many job descriptions for emergency management will also call for, at a minimum, a multi-tasker who is detail oriented with the ability to plan thoroughly, communicate effectively, and to lead and coordinate during disasters (CareerPlanner.com). To be sure, individuals who meet these criteria may do well in general; however, since emergency management directors tend to be typically college educated white males with an above-average salary job with some expectation of job security, more is required to be most effective. Additionally, traits that are equally important but hardly mentioned include empathy, humility, and compassion. It is when these traits are in play, the emergency manager has the gumption and ability to get closer to meeting federal civil rights mandate that calls for disaster plans to address the needs of all "in an equitable and impartial manner, without discrimination on the grounds of race, color, religion, [national origin], sex, age, disability, English proficiency, or economic status" (FEMA, *Office of equal rights*).

Using the scenario at the beginning of this chapter, an emergency manager should seek to peel back all the layers and ask probing questions. Just how many individuals have the time, energy, interest, and resources to attend a civic league meeting? How many property owners or renters are challenged every day to meet their most basic needs? How many struggle to pay their bills or put food on the table with income levels in or near the poverty range? In the face of such direct and immediate economic hurdles, how realistic is it to expect them to carry flood insurance—a cost which is on the rise (Bagenstose et al.)—for an incident that may or may not happen this year or the next? Without flood insurance, would their repetitive damages appear on a map? Without flood insurance, would they be eligible for Increased Cost of Compliance (ICC) funds to assist with critical repairs (the answer is no). Without flood insurance, would they be eligible for FEMA mitigation programs? And, what choices—or circumstances—led them to reside in such vulnerable areas in the first place?

One resource one may use to better understand the makeup of a community is the US Census Bureau that offers a topic area useful and specific to Emergency

Management (U.S. Census Bureau, n.d.). The tool's pre-incident information includes data related to demographics and population. Available is information with a direct correlation to an individual's ability to prepare and respond to disasters such as poverty, vehicle access, cultural and language barriers as well as disabilities and seniors. The Centers for Disease Control and Prevention (CDC) offers another valuable online resource that consumes the Census information and then analyzes the data by census tract using "15 social factors, including poverty, lack of vehicle access, and crowded housing, and groups them into four related themes." The end result is known as the Social Vulnerability Index (SVI) (CDC, 2022). According to the CDC, SVI information can assist to:

- Estimate the amount of needed supplies like food, water, medicine, and bedding.
- Help decide how many emergency personnel are required to assist people.
- Identify areas in need of emergency shelters.
- Plan the best way to evacuate people, accounting for those who have special needs, such as people without vehicles, the elderly, or people who do not understand English well.
- Identify communities that will need continued support to recover following an emergency or natural disaster.

Suffice it to say, poverty is a glaring factor, which plays a role in an individual's circumstance and a significant barrier to preparedness. After all, there is no choice when the "options" are to purchase supplies for a disaster kit or buy food for the next meal. In order to obtain more information on the levels and locations of poverty in a community, a trip to the local food bank as well as the school district's department of nutrition may be in order. Both are informed as to where the greatest need exists and both leveraged that information and performed heroically keeping people fed throughout the Coronavirus 2019 pandemic. Food Banks throughout the nation maintain food insecurity ("food deserts") maps reflecting "a substantial number or share of residents with low levels of access to retail outlets selling healthy and affordable foods" (US Department of Agriculture [USDA], *Mapping food deserts in the United States*) in their respective communities. Many public schools participate in the USDA's Community Eligibility Provision (CEP) program (USDA, *Community eligibility provision*) that makes available to school students meals free of charge if not at a reduced rate. Of course, children are not the only members of a community who rely on others for their nutritional needs; a community may have a large number of Supplemental Nutrition Assistance Programs (SNAP, formerly known as Food Stamps) recipients (USDA, 2021). What is critical for an Emergency Manager to understand about this type of assistance is that most programs pay around the beginning of the month and are not intended to make the recipient entirely whole. For example, the Standards of Assistance for the Temporary Assistance for Needy Families (TANF) are set at 90% of need. Said differently, the amount of benefits clients receive is set by the State at a level that will not cover all their basic needs—standards that have not kept up with the true cost of living. So, even if a disaster were to occur when a client just received their benefits for the month, they would likely be unable to cover evacuation costs. It is also important to understand poverty numbers will not tell the whole story. There are people employed in positions essential to America's prosperity (Shipler) who earn more income than the Federal Poverty Level (US Department of Health and Human Services) "but not enough to afford basic household necessities" and are equally vulnerable. To know this larger, hidden segment of the population, you must know Asset Limited, Income Constrained, Employed (ALICE).

ALICE is a tool developed by the United Way in partnership with a number of organizations to help paint a more accurate picture of community vulnerability. This includes households who are challenged to make ends meet during blue sky days with low wage, hourly wage work, and minimal job security. They also have little to no flexibility in their schedule and likely no insurance or savings. Any impact on their job, whether an unexpected transportation or care-giver issue or a larger-scale incident, will have immediate and significant impacts on the household (United Way, *Research center – national overview*). In fact, as stated in their financial hardship study:

> ALICE households are more vulnerable during natural disasters as they often live-in communities with fewer resources, and housing that is more susceptible to flooding, fire, and other hazards. With no financial cushion, ALICE workers struggle to repair damage, recover from illness, and pay ongoing bills. At the same time, ALICE workers are essential to disaster recovery efforts in both infrastructure repair and health care, and they are often forced to choose between caring for their families and ensuing community recovery. All of these costs are added to the increased risk of physical harm ALICE families face if they cannot afford to flee an oncoming natural disaster or take necessary precautions during a public health crisis.
>
> *ibid.*

Dr. J Marshall Shepherd states in his June 2021 Forbes article: "everyone is exposed to extreme weather and climate events, but it is inaccurate to say that outcomes are equal" (Shepherd, 2021). Volumes have been written about the roles equity issues play in where an individual lives. And, history is clear about the institutional and generational injustices, which also played in the availability of affordable housing options—often in less desirable areas more prone to hazards like flooding. Of course, the focus should not be on flooding alone. Other less desirable areas of a community may be near railroads, which transports hazardous product (Wood, 2019), hazardous waste or superfund sites (Bendix, 2018), or near facilities where hazardous chemicals are stored in large quantities (Kennedy, 2020). Emergency managers and members of the community should be aware of this latter threat due to the Emergency Planning and Community Right-to-Know Act (EPCRA) (Environmental Protection Agency). It is important to understand, these circumstances have a direct correlation to the decisions made in the face of a disaster. Old Dominion University's Virginia Modeling, Analysis and Simulation Center is a nationally recognized leader known for researching behaviors tied to disaster situations. Some of their work involve such studies for the Hampton Roads Regional Catastrophic Planning Team. When considering vulnerable populations and flood loss in their 2014 document, *Unraveling the evacuation behavior of the medically fragile population: findings from hurricane Irene*, their research shows that for many population behaviors related to where someone chooses to live, they are based on how risk is perceived, and those perceptions are further shaped by several factors such as previous experiences (Ng et al., 2014). Even if an individual has experienced loss during a previous storm, and they perceive the risk to be great, their ability to act in a more safe and responsible manner is conditioned by a number of "issues of equity" *such as* "access, resources, knowledge, wellbeing, medical, fragility, social networks, efficacy, etc." Case in point: Individuals who rely on low-end hourly wages may be less inclined to evacuate ahead of a storm due to lack of resources or their employer needs them to stay and work. They have no choice. These are not situations in which most would choose to be. As previously stated, the location in which someone chooses to reside may be no choice at all. In many instances, there are some deeply rooted issues that deserve time in study to learn and understand and could fill many volumes to explain.

Another incident gaining in familiarity and frequency with a changing climate is excessive heat—the greatest cause of weather-related fatalities over the 10- and 30-year average. Mr. Eric Klineberg wrote about a wide range of reasons why this is so, particularly among the most vulnerable communities, in his excellent book about the 1995 heat wave, which took the lives of over 700 Chicagoans, *Heat Wave: A Social Autopsy of Disaster in Chicago*. Klineberg found "Heat wave deaths were concentrated in the low-income, elderly, African-American, and violent regions of the metropolis" (Klinenberg, 2015). Furthermore, high-crime was a reason many elderly residents lived in isolation—residents who today may rely on home-delivered meals from organizations like Meals on Wheels—and rarely leaving their home if at all. These individuals must be remembered during post-disaster commodity distribution efforts. Dr. Michael Allen, Associate Professor and Geography Program Director at Old Dominion University, has been researching the why's and how's behind excessive heat and phenomena in urban areas known as "heat islands" due to the non-pervious land cover as well as lack of tree canopy. He creates a *Heat Index Vulnerability Map* "by combining temperature, land cover, and poverty data …" (Person, 2021). He also found and shares the correlation of "Red-Lining" and "areas [which] experience warmer temperatures when compared to other neighborhoods." What is Red Lining? "Red-Lining" was a federal housing policy which denied people, mostly Black and Brown communities, access to home financing mortgages. The Home Owners' Loan Corporation demarcated neighborhoods based on "grades"—A ("Best," outlined in green) "Still Desirable" (B, outlined in blue), "Definitely Declining" (C, outlined in yellow), to "Hazardous" (D, outlined in red) (ibid.). While this occurred in the past, the University of Richmond's *Not Even Past* map shows affects continue to be felt today (Digital Scholarship Lab and the National Community Reinvestment Coalition). This important work also makes known the following: "Where people live will likely correlate with their exposure to health-promoting resources and opportunities (i.e., access to quality food, recreation, healthcare, etc.) as well as exposure to health-damaging threats (i.e., environmental pollutants, poor housing quality, etc.)" (ibid.). All of these issues discussed are tied to an individual's ability to be prepared for a disaster. Fortunately, the CDC has two programs designed to address them: Community Health Assessments and Health Improvement Plans (CHA/CHIP) (CDC, 2018).

Many areas vulnerable to acute shocks may also be exposed to chronic stresses which, sadly, make it possible to predict a shortened lifespan. But there is a solution. Just as a Natural Hazards Mitigation Plan identifies a community's hazards, risks, vulnerabilities, and action items, so too, does the CDC's CHA and CHIP. The CHA is

> a systematic examination of the health status indicators for a given population that is used to identify key problems and assets in a community. The ultimate goal of a community health assessment is to develop strategies to address the community's health needs and identified issues.
>
> *CDC, 2018*

This is accomplished by focusing on "[l]ong-standing systemic health, social, and economic inequities [which] have put some members of racial and ethnic minority groups, as well as people with lower incomes, at increased risk of getting COVID-19 or experiencing severe illness, regardless of age." In other words, the CDC's social determinants of health (CDC, 2020). The CHIP is then "a long-term, systematic effort to address public health problems based on the results of community health assessment activities and the community health improvement process. A plan is typically updated every three to five years" (CDC, 2018). This Assessment and Improvement Plan approach is critical to identify and remedy chronic health-related issues. And, unless such chronic issues are addressed, individual preparedness will not be realized and thus emergency managers should be engaged and otherwise support these efforts. Moreover, it is also the opportunity to build trust within the community during blue skies, which is so important during gray skies.

"The poor and impoverished will be ok; that's what FEMA is for, right?" This may be what many people believe. However, federal assistance of any kind is not a guarantee. In fact, a chain of events must take place first to get to that point. Under the Stafford Act, states must review and assess damage to declare a state of emergency and officially request federal recovery assistance. If requirements are met, the President may approve the request for aid by declaring an emergency declaration or a major disaster declaration. There is a significant difference between the two with the Major Disaster declaration being more comprehensive. Programs can include disaster housing and unemployment assistance, benefits and distribution (aka Disaster Supplemental Nutrition Assistance Program or D-SNAP) (DisasterAssistance.gov), food commodities and transportation assistance. It is important to understand, however, these programs are merely authorized; the President decides which will be included as part of the declaration that is why it is imperative for local emergency managers to communicate the need in their situation reports and initial damage assessments. It is also critical to understand FEMA assistance is supplemental and not intended to make anyone completely whole, whereas flood insurance is. Put differently, the National Flood Insurance Program suggests just 1 inch of water can cause $25,000 in damages to a home (FEMA, *The cost of flooding*). Those with flood insurance will receive compensation to cover replacement costs for damages and destroyed property based on their claim and documentation. Individuals who rely on FEMA assistance and are eligible may receive a disaster loan that must be repaid over time with interest—an additional expenditure to an already-strapped budget (FEMA, *FACT SHEET*). Of course, the inability to pay bills when due results in cascading affects such as penalty fees and weakening credit scores, which result in more down-range consequences.

Strategies to Help Achieve Resiliency

Understand not everyone shares the same experiences and world view as you. There can be much benefit to spending time in reading and understanding history and especially local history. Spending time talking, and more importantly listening, to people throughout the community is also key. As you go down this path of greater awareness, do your best to challenge and otherwise dispel any preconceived stereotypes you may have. One way to accomplish this is to participate in the United Way's Poverty Simulation (United Way, *Breaking the cycle – Formstack*). This simulation will quickly help the participant to realize vulnerable circumstances are not necessarily synonymous with vulnerable people.

Understand individual and household preparedness is not always a choice. While a great degree of emergency management outreach information is designed to encourage good choices, rarely are they geared toward addressing an individual's most pressing needs. Referring to Maslow's Hierarchy of Needs, a person's most basic needs must be addressed before there is a chance to address any self-fulfillment needs like disaster preparedness. As such, it is important to recognize that current disparities in health and well-being that are present today will be amplified during incidents for which there is no notice. An emergency manager should not only be aware of areas of poverty, but the presence of the "working poor" as provided by ALICE. Additionally, emergency managers should leverage the CDC's SVI and support efforts related to the CHA and CHIP—efforts which if done during blue-skies, will serve to build trust within the community. Lastly, it is helpful to have a list of resources in the community and surrounding areas available to assist with an individual's or household's greatest needs. Norfolk, Virginia's Emergency Preparedness and Response's "Community Resources and Connections" has an example of this resource directory (Norfolk Emergency Preparedness and Response). Failure to understand and assist with these needs in the mitigation and planning phases will result in preventable layers of surprise and complexity during an actual incident.

Ensure inclusion in your emergency management program. In other words, consult with people who do not look or live like you! Step outside your social circles and meet people where they already are! Instead of planning special preparedness events, partner with your local social/human services and take part in their events which people in need already attend. Furthermore, consider establishing an advisory board or strategic committee—a group of trusted leaders representing various cultures and abilities throughout the community who can not only offer input but also bring legitimacy in areas where trust is lacking. These partners can also serve as force multipliers for emergency management efforts and messaging. Other ideas are available in a collaboration between The Resilience Partnership Network, FEMA, and the National Oceanic Atmospheric Administration (NOAA) entitled *Building Alliances for Equitable Resilience* (April 2021).

Summary

The emergency management profession is one lacking in diversity and inclusion and requires a determined approach to address the needs of the entire community. In fact, regardless the disaster scenario, the more one investigates, the more one understands the impacts of past decisions and realizes current plans and policies rarely address those with the greatest need. Fortunately, tools and resources are available to help today's emergency manager expand their world view and better understand the vulnerabilities that exist throughout the community. Not just what those vulnerabilities are and where, but how they came to be and what can be done to do the greatest good for the greatest number in your community *with the greatest need*. Emergency managers are mandated by law to address the needs of all "in an equitable and impartial manner, without discrimination on the grounds of race, color, religion, [national origin], sex, age, disability, English proficiency, or economic status." More importantly, it is the right thing to do.

Conclusion

Disasters have shown time and again that a one-size fits all approach does not work for community preparedness. Some members of a community are well-resourced with options to prevent loss of life resulting from an impending threat or at least navigate potential loss of property. It is for this group so many plans are written; however, if the emergency manager is willing to look outside their own world view, they will find that many others are casualties of circumstance with no choice at all. It is the latter who are most vulnerable to disaster and for whom particular attention must be paid. In the words of Damian Barr in May 2020, "We are not all in the same boat. We are all in the same storm. Some are on super-yachts. Some have just the one oar."

Discussion/Review Questions

1. What are you willing to do to broaden your world view, to dispel stereotypes and better empathize with others?
2. What organizations exist in your community to help reach various demographics?
3. What can you do to help individuals meet their most basic needs (and build trust) so their self-fulfillment needs to eventually be addressed?
4. What goals or objectives should be added to your hazard mitigation plan, recovery plan, and/or your community's capital improvement plan to address these generational issues of vulnerability?

References

Bagenstose, K., Pulver, D.V., & Crowe, K. (2021, February 23). *Flood-prone homeowners could see major rate hikes in FEMA flood insurance changes, new study finds.* USA Today. Retrieved September 29, 2021, from www.usatoday.com/in-depth/news/investigations/2021/02/21/fema-flood-insurance-rates-could-spike-some-new-study-shows/6764469002/.

Bendix, A. (2018, October 31). San Francisco's planned $8 billion neighborhood has a radio-active past, and it may put people at a higher risk of cancer than experts thought. Business Insider. www.businessinsider.com/san-francisco-shipyard-navy-cancer-risk-2018-10.

CareerPlanner.com. (n.d.). Emergency management specialist job description. *Emergency management specialist job description, duties and jobs – Part 1.* Retrieved September 29, 2021, from https://job-descriptions.careerplanner.com/Emergency-Management-Specialists.cfm.

Centers for Disease Control and Prevention. (2018, July 24). *CDC – assessment and plans – community health assessment – STLT gateway.* Centers for Disease Control and Prevention. www.cdc.gov/publichealthgateway/cha/plan.html.

Centers for Disease Control and Prevention. (2020, October 23). *CDC – social determinants of health – STLT gateway.* Centers for Disease Control and Prevention. www.cdc.gov/publichealthgateway/sdoh/index.html.

Centers for Disease Control and Prevention. (2022). *Social Vulnerability Index (SVI) interactive mapping.* Centers for Disease Control and Prevention. Retrieved February 16, 2022. www.atsdr.cdc.gov/placeandhealth/svi/index.html

Data USA. (n.d.). Emergency management directors. Retrieved September 29, 2021, from https://datausa.io/profile/soc/emergency-management-directors#:~:text=Demographic%20information%20on%20Emergency%20management,White%20(Non%2DHispanic).

Digital Scholarship Lab and the National Community Reinvestment Coalition, "Not even past: social vulnerability and the legacy of redlining," *American panorama*, eds. Robert K. Nelson and Edward L. Ayers. Retrieved February 16, 2022, from https://dsl.richmond. edu/socialvulnerability.

DisasterAssistance.gov. (n.d.). *Disaster Supplemental Nutrition Assistance Program (D-SNAP).* Disaster Supplemental Nutrition Assistance Program (D-SNAP). Retrieved September 29, 2021, from www.disasterassistance.gov/get-assistance/forms-of-assistance/5769.

Environmental Protection Agency. (n.d.). *Emergency Planning and Community Right-to-Know Act (EPCRA).* EPA. Retrieved September 29, 2021, from www.epa.gov/epcra.

Federal Emergency Management Agency (FEMA). (n.d.). FACT SHEET: FEMA *individual assistance is not a substitute for in*surance. FEMA.gov. Retrieved September 29, 2021, from www.fema.gov/news-release/20200220/fact-sheet-fema-individual-assistance-not-substitute-insurance.

Federal Emergency Management Agency (FEMA). (n.d.). Office of equal rights. FEMA. gov. Retrieved September 29, 2021, from www.fema.gov/about/offices/equal-rights.

Federal Emergency Management Association (FEMA). (n.d.). *The cost of flooding.* FloodSmart. Retrieved September 29, 2021, from www.floodsmart.gov/flood-insurance-cost/ calculator.

Kennedy, M. (2020, January 24). At *least 2 people killed in massive industrial explosion in Houston.* NPR. www.npr.org/2020/01/24/799217399/at-least-2-people-killed-in-massive-industrial-explosion-in-houston.

Klinenberg, E. (2015). *Heat wave: a social autopsy of disaster in Chicago.* Chicago, IL: The University of Chicago Press. p. 3.

Ng, M.W., Behr, J., & Diaz, R. (2014, April 19). *Unraveling the evacuation behavior of the medically fragile POPULATION: findings from Hurricane Irene.* Transportation Research Part A: Policy and Practice. Retrieved September 29, 2021, from www.sciencedirect.com/ science/article/abs/pii/S0965856414000809.

Norfolk Emergency Preparedness and Response. (n.d.). *Be prepared.* Be Prepared | City of Norfolk, Virginia – Official Website. Retrieved September 29, 2021, from www.norfolk. gov/3987/Be-Prepared.

Person. (2021, June 10). *Norfolk heat vulnerability.* ArcGIS StoryMaps. Retrieved September 29, 2021, from https://storymaps.arcgis.com/stories/7cde13a422504a0682ec9c2de b18c4b6.

Shepherd, M. (2021, June 5). *Equity in weather warnings is a hot topic but the issue is much deeper.* Forbes. www-forbes-com.cdn.ampproject.org/c/s/www.forbes.com/sites/ marshallshepherd/2021/06/04/equity-in-weather-warnings-is-a-hot-topic-but-the-issue-is-much-deeper/amp/.

Shipler, D. K. (2009). *The working poor: invisible in America.* New York: Vintage Books. p. 300.

United Way. (n.d.). *Breaking the cycle – Formstack.* Workplace Productivity & Automation Tools. Retrieved September 29, 2021, from https://unitedway.formstack.com/forms/ breaking_the_cycle.

United Way. (n.d.). *Research center – national overview.* unitedforalice. Retrieved September 29, 2021, from https://unitedforalice.org/national-overview.

US Bureau of Labor Statistics. (2021, September 13). *Emergency management directors: occupational outlook handbook.* US Bureau of Labor Statistics. Retrieved September 29, 2021, from www.bls.gov/ooh/management/emergency-management-directors.htm.

US Census Bureau. (n.d.). *Emergency management.* Census.gov. Retrieved September 29, 2021, from www.census.gov/topics/preparedness.html.

US Department of Agriculture. (n.d.). *Community eligibility provision*. USDA. Retrieved September 29, 2021, from www.fns.usda.gov/cn/community-eligibility-provision.

US Department of Agriculture. (n.d.). *Mapping food deserts in the United States*. USDA ERS – Data Feature: Mapping Food Deserts in the U.S. Retrieved September 29, 2021, from www.ers.usda.gov/amber-waves/2011/december/data-feature-mapping-food-deserts-in-the-us/.

US Department of Agriculture. (2021, August 16). *Supplemental Nutrition Assistance Program (SNAP)*. USDA. Retrieved September 29, 2021, from www.fns.usda.gov/snap/supplemental-nutrition-assistance-program.

US Department of Health and Human Services. (n.d.). *2021 Poverty guidelines*. ASPE. Retrieved September 29, 2021, from https://aspe.hhs.gov/2021-poverty-guidelines.

Wood, L. (2019, March 9). Graniteville continues to recover almost 15 years after train Crash, chlorine leak. AP News. Retrieved September 29, 2021, from https://apnews.com/033ae27086874317b67d3d72a6e510ec.

9

PUBLIC WORKS: A PARTNER TO BUILD MORE EQUITABLE COMMUNITIES

James W. Patteson

Introduction

Public Works Organizations (PWOs) are committed to enhancing the quality of life in our communities through building and maintaining America's infrastructure and through providing the services citizens rely on every day. High-quality, well-maintained infrastructure is the backbone of any successful society. Public Works professionals are responsible for designing, implementing, managing, and maintaining trillions of dollars worth of infrastructure. The transportation, water supply, sewage treatment, flood control, public facilities, electric transmission, and communication infrastructure are the underpinnings of our national security, our quality of life, and our economic competitiveness in the world. PWOs are at the front lines of responding to natural disasters and building more resilient communities. They are the quiet force carrying out tasks, small and large, that keep our communities thriving. The current challenge is to ensure the benefits and impacts of these services are equitably shared across the community.

Racial and social equity is often viewed through the dramatic lens of public safety and the criminal justice system. Headlines are dominated by the tragic stories of George Floyd, Breonna Taylor, and Ahmaud Arbery. The Black Lives Matter movement advocates against police brutality toward Black people, racially motivated violence, and unfair treatment in the criminal justice system. This movement has sparked a larger review of programs and services offered by government and private enterprise. Government agencies are evaluating programs and examining root causes of inequities in their communities to better understand how they can be addressed. Local leaders know that it will take a shared effort across all government agencies, working in collaboration with the communities

DOI: 10.4324/9781003186076-10

they serve, to create a more equitable society. PWOs are an important partner in this effort.

The Built Environment's Impact on Equity

Human health, the natural environment, and infrastructure are intrinsically linked. Dr. Richard Jackson, MD, University of California, Los Angeles, a leading expert in the relationship between health and environment, posits that the environment in which people live is at the core of public health. In his book, "Building Healthy Communities," Dr. Jackson describes the importance of this linkage (Jackson, 2012). Community health scores are higher in areas with better environmental resources and infrastructure. A jurisdiction with pedestrian friendly walkways, bike trails, easy access to parks and recreation, access to multimodal transportation systems, and clean air and water are much healthier than those without. Dr. Jackson stresses, given the strong correlation between human health and the environment, it is important to equitably share these resources across the full community.

Dr. Steven Woolf, MD, Masters Public Health, studies the disparity in these resources within communities. In his report, "Getting Ahead – The Uneven Opportunity Landscape in Northern Virginia," he states that traditional health care accounts for only 10%–20% of community health, while human behaviors and the environment account for the rest (Steven H. Woolf, 2017). Health care tends to be a reactionary system, while behaviors and environment are predeterminants. Improvements in the environment will support improvements in public health, behaviors, and other socioeconomic factors. Dr. Woolf finds, through analyzing census data, that there is a large disparity in community health indicators that directly correlates with socioeconomic and racial demographical data. The poorest communities tend to amass disadvantages that negatively impact access to opportunities; crime rates are higher, infrastructure systems are in disrepair, safe access to parks is challenging, and transportation systems do not provide an easy connection to jobs. These communities are disproportionately populated by people of color. Dr. Jackson's and Dr. Woolf's research shows the impact of the built environment on human outcomes and equity. To create an equal opportunity for success, PWOs must consider these factors as they build infrastructure and provide services throughout their communities.

Public Works' Role in Providing Infrastructure

PWOs, working in partnership with parks and planning agencies, are at the front lines of building the infrastructure that connects citizens to opportunities. The challenge for PWOs is to plan and build infrastructure in a manner that benefits all members of the community. Do the roads and transportation systems connect or divide neighborhoods? Are safe and adequate bike and pedestrian facilities provided in all neighborhoods? Do public transportation systems equitably connect all citizens to jobs, schools, parks, and other amenities? How are maintenance and reinvestment decisions made? Is there bias in how noxious uses such as landfills, wastewater treatment plants, and other industrial operations are sited? To provide an equal opportunity for everyone to access the resources of the community, it is important for PWOs to ask these questions and review their work through an equity perspective.

The role of PWOs in building equitable infrastructure cannot be understated. According to the Congressional Budget Office, state and local governments outspend the federal government on infrastructure in every category of project. Public infrastructure capital investment equated to $174B in 2017, with nearly 60% from state and local resources. Professional planners and engineers in PWOs at the state and local level are making the recommendations on design standards, reinvestment levels, location of facilities, and levels of service.

To ensure equitable outcomes for all communities, infrastructure investment decisions need to be based not only on the financial and engineering data but also on the socioeconomic data. Solutions need to provide equitable access to opportunities across all communities and address negative impacts of previous actions. Engaging the full community, especially historically underrepresented parts of the community, is important to guide this work in an equitable manner.

A History of Bias

Too often in United States' history, infrastructure created barriers for certain communities rather than connections. Imagine that your home is a quarter mile from downtown where you work and buy groceries. One day a new highway is built to serve suburban commuters and your ability to walk downtown is now blocked. The nearest overpass is miles away. The public transportation is limited in your neighborhood. The streetlights at the bus stop and along the sidewalk are out and your walk home from the one bus stop is dark and unsafe. Situations like this have occurred in cities across the country and have disadvantaged certain neighborhoods. It is important to understand this history and implement measures to mitigate the impacts of past practices and improve equity in our communities.

Infrastructure decisions have a large impact, are long lasting, and cannot simply be changed. Once a road or a bridge is built, or a landfill or wastewater treatment plant is sited, it cannot be easily redone. This infrastructure will last 50–100 years and hardwires certain conditions into our communities. A town's development patterns and economy are directly tied to large infrastructure investments. For instance, Main Street retailers in towns across the United States have struggled after the construction of a highway bypass. While the bypass was intended to ease congestion, local communities experienced unintended negative consequences from these projects. Highway travelers and large retailers located along the bypass benefited while smaller businesses located downtown were disadvantaged.

Future infrastructure decisions are often based on previous decisions. High investments in public infrastructure will improve real estate values and attract private investment which can result in a highly desirable location. The opposite is also true. A lack of investment in public infrastructure will result in deteriorated conditions which can lead to declining real estate values, a lack of private investment, and community blight. For these reasons, public investments need to be made with a holistic understanding of the impacts of those investments. Historically, in the United States, infrastructure decisions have been made that disadvantaged our communities along racial and socioeconomic lines.

Bias in Public Transportation

Mobility is a fundamental societal need. How people get to work, school, and parks, and how people obtain basic needs like groceries and health care is core to their quality of life. The transportation systems and land use planning decisions in the United States have well documented historical biases. Decisions on road alignments, bus service, mass transit station locations, and location and access to parks and other community amenities have disadvantaged communities of color.

In her article, *White Men's Roads through Black Men's Homes: Advancing Racial Equity Through Highway Reconstruction*, Deborah N. Archer explores the structural and institutional racism that shaped the interstate highway system (Archer, 2020). The construction of the interstate system disproportionately impacted communities of color. Ms. Archer provides several examples including Interstate 94 in St. Paul, Minnesota, that displaced one-seventh of the city's Black residents, and Interstate 579 in Pittsburgh that decimated and separated the Hill District, a Black community, from Pittsburgh's thriving downtown. Ms. Archer recommends applying a racial and social equity lens to highway reinvestment decisions to correct for earlier inequitable actions.

There are also historical biases in decisions about transportation investment and designs of public transportation systems. The Transportation Trust Fund, which cities and towns rely on for local projects, is heavily directed toward road projects. Less than 20% of this funding is dedicated to public transportation projects, leaving these systems woefully underfunded (Epanty, 2018). A study conducted by the American Public Transportation Association, *Who Rides Public Transportation*, shows that 60% of riders are individuals of color (Hugh M. Clark, 2017). The mass transit systems, routes, and stations are also designed predominately for the commuter and often do not provide easy access for residents of low-income communities to access local jobs and needed services. The combination of underinvestment and inequitable design decisions creates mobility challenges for residents in poorer communities. To provide equal opportunities for success, transportation system designs need to address the needs of the full community.

Bias in Infrastructure—Case Studies

East Side Story

A study conducted by Stephan Heblich, Alex Trew, and Yanos Zylberberg found that, in the Western Hemisphere, the east sides of formerly industrialized cities are more likely to have poorer populations (Heblich et al., 2021). The cause is related to prevailing easterly winds and the location of industrial coal burning smokestacks. The disamenity of polluted air caused neighborhood sorting as more affluent residents were able to move to cleaner air environments on the west side of the smokestacks while poorer residents were not. The study found that the neighborhood sorting outlasted the pollution. The east side communities suffered other negative factors that define the desirability of neighborhoods including high crime rates, low quality schools, lack of quality infrastructure, and fewer public amenities. The impacts of this neighborhood sorting compounded over time to create a gap between the haves and the have nots over multiple generations. While the pollution has mostly disappeared over the last hundred years, the negative outcomes to these communities have lingered.

Islands of Disadvantage in Northern Virginia

Dr. Woolf analyzed two adjoining census tracts in Fairfax County, Virginia, an affluent suburb of Washington, DC (Woolf, 2017). He found that while the county, by most objective measures, is a great place to live and work, opportunities for success are not equally shared across all communities. Health outcomes varied widely with an 18-year difference in life expectancy based on socioeconomic status and the environmental conditions in one's neighborhood. Coined "islands of disadvantage," these poorer communities, which are populated disproportionately by people of color, suffer multiple challenges. There are stark differences in educational attainment for the adults, early education attendance of the children, income, language proficiency, and life span. Dr. Woolf's research suggests a strong linkage between economic opportunity, health, and the built environment within communities. He recommends thoughtful consideration of investment into these areas to reverse historical trends and change the islands of disadvantage into communities of opportunity.

Inequity in Seattle Streetlight Services

Often, there is unintentional bias built into the design of our systems. The City of Seattle learned this about their streetlight replacement program. After a series of shootings in the southeast area of the city, the mayor of Seattle and city staff took a bus tour of the area (Nelson, 2020). The mayor wanted to understand the conditions in the neighborhood where five young men of color had died over the previous three months. The demographics of the area were 80% people of color and over 50% low income. The city officials noticed that many of the streetlights were out. They understood that streetlights were an important component of safe neighborhoods.

City staff used a social equity tool kit to analyze how work orders were processed and learned that streetlight replacements were complaint based. A resident needed to call the city to report an outage and the city public works department would respond. The problem, the city learned, was that there were numerous barriers for the residents in this neighborhood to access this system. The barriers included a lack of trust of government, language barriers, and not understanding who to call and how to report. The unintended outcome of the self-reporting system was a disproportionate number of outages in the poorest communities in Seattle, which resulted in less safe streets and higher crime rates.

The solution was simple. Seattle shifted to a scheduled replacement program based on lighting zones. The solution not only provided greater equity, but it was also more efficient and saved Seattle money. The city also expanded its review of other complaint-based systems to improve how they equitably deploy resources for pothole repairs, blighted property complaints, and police resource assignments.

What Can Be Done—Case Studies

King County, Washington

In 2016, King County published its first Equity and Social Justice (ESJ) Strategic Plan, to ensure fairer outcomes (King County, 2016). The plan identifies specific objectives. One of the objectives focuses on how investments in infrastructure systems can advance the county's ESJ objectives. The plan directs the use of a pro-equity process that includes: an equity impact review; a targeted allocation of resources toward impacted communities; an extensive engagement effort to hear from, understand, and respond to impacted communities; and regional collaboration. To improve equity in infrastructure investment, three specific goals are provided in the plan:

- Goal 1—Infrastructure system master plans (including line of business and other strategic planning processes) include clear objectives to advance ESJ that are informed by and sensitive to priority populations and key affected parties.
- Goal 2—Capital development policy, budgets, portfolios, and programs are developed in accordance with community equity priorities, informed by a perspective on historic and existing inequities, and include a description of their contribution to improving equity in community conditions.
- Goal 3—Activities and responsibilities for pro-equity progress are clear and defined at the Department, Division, and Section levels.

The ESJ plan has created a new focus on how services are provided to the community. The King County Solid Waste Division (SWD), for example, created its own objectives to align with the ESJ plan. The SWD planning effort involved a review of employee recruiting and development, rate structures, contracting procedures, customer service, and community engagement. The resultant plan included the development of a low-income discount program for disposing of waste; an assessment of recycling center availability to low-income communities; and the recommendation for improving the diversity of the solid waste advisory committees.

Fairfax County, Virginia

In 2017, One Fairfax, a joint racial and social equity policy, was adopted by the Fairfax County Board of Supervisors and the School Board (Fairfax County, 2017). The policy acknowledged that inequities exist in the county that must be addressed through consideration of equity in all planning and decision-making. County leadership recognized that all agencies needed to be engaged in this important work. Equity leads were identified for each department. They were provided with specific training to understand key equity concepts and were guided through an equity impact planning process. Every department was required to develop an equity action plan in line with the One Fairfax Policy. The equity leads became the champions in their respective departments to identify disparities in the outcomes of their services and to develop strategies to address those areas.

One exercise undertaken by the Department of Public Works and Environmental Services was to evaluate the percentage of tree coverage across the county. The county has a long-standing goal of 50% tree cover as part of its environmental vision. The DPWES Geographic Information System manager overlaid the tree cover layer with the community vulnerability index map and discovered a direct negative correlation between tree cover and vulnerable communities. This information is now being used by the county's Urban Forestry Division to target tree planting initiatives.

Tools to Improve Equity

Engagement

One of the most important ways to ensure equity in an organization's efforts is to engage diverse voices. The goal is to listen and better understand the different needs and perspectives of community members and to codevelop solutions that address those needs. One size fits all solutions do not work well given the complexities of our diverse communities. To provide equitable opportunities for success, solutions need to be tailored to meet the varied needs of different communities. Authentic and consistent engagement is necessary to build trust with the community and to accomplish this goal.

PWOs are utilizing new approaches to community engagement to improve public trust and build better projects. The Metropolitan Sewerage District (MSD) in Madison, Wisconsin utilized an extensive public outreach and stakeholder engagement process to work with surrounding businesses and residents to replace a 40-year-old sewage pump station (Institute for Sustainable Infrastructure, 2018). The $4.3M upgrades were needed due to the age of the facility and to increase capacity for the growing community. By engaging the community and many different stakeholders, unique partnerships were formed, and the project was able to achieve local conservation goals and provide several amenities. The project, located along the shore of Lake Mendota, included a multi-use trail, public restrooms, bike repair station, and an aquatic invasive species boat wash. The project also includes numerous environmental features including solar panels, a green roof, porous pavement, and a bioswale to treat stormwater runoff. Through engaging the community and understanding their needs, MSD was able to deliver a project that met the sewer needs for the region while also addressing local needs.

To ensure engagement is equitable, there needs to be an effort to hear from historically underrepresented voices and to remove barriers to participation. In Fairfax County, Virginia, a community-wide strategic plan was developed in 2020 (Fairfax County, 2020). A driving principle of the planning process was to engage the community in an equitable fashion and to hear from a diversity of voices. County staff employed a number of creative strategies to accomplish this goal. Events were held at the local university. High school history and social studies teachers were asked to survey students. Surveys were sent to parents through the Parent Teacher Association. Community input sessions were held in different communities at different times to capture shift workers. Events were held at the senior center. Transportation, childcare, and translation services were provided at events. Community influencers were recruited to help spread the word and provide input on the plan. Collection of information also included demographic data so responses could be sorted to understand if there were different issues based on these factors. Through this effort, Fairfax was better able to target strategies based upon the needs of different communities.

Engaging staff within PWOs is also important. The diverse voices internal to the organization need to be engaged to develop a shared goal of serving the full community in an equitable way.

Education and Exposure

Social equity and how it applies to departmental goals is a new concept for many agencies. Spending the time to train staff and create a shared understanding of equity issues in the community and everyone's role in addressing these issues is important. There are numerous training programs to accomplish this work.

One very effective tool is to conduct an equity tour in one's community. Visit neighborhoods with high vulnerability scores and those with low scores. Visit the homeless shelter and speak with the counselors and clients. Visit the food bank. Review the demographic and other socioeconomic data in these areas to better understand differences between neighborhoods. Supplement this experiential training with equity impact training to determine what intervention strategies have the greatest impact and how to plan and implement these measures.

The higher education community is incorporating social equity content in courses across all different majors. The American Society of Engineering Education (ASEE) is a leading organization that supports higher education practitioners in the field of engineering. ASEE's core value is, "Excellence, engagement, innovation, integrity, diversity and inclusion" (American Society for Engineering Education, 2021). To support this value, ASEE seeks to cultivate an inclusive community, value the contributions of all stakeholders, promote diversity, and model equity and inclusion. At a 2019 presentation at ASEE's Collaborative Network for Engineering and Computing Diversity (NECD) event, Dr. Dianne Grayce Hendricks, University of Washington, Celina Gunnarsson, Massachusetts Institute of Technology, and Camille Birch, University of Washington stressed the need for a curriculum that integrates engineering and social equity (Dr. Dianne Grayce Hendrics, 2019). Their presentation recognized that many engineering students lack exposure to social justice themes in their technical coursework. Students need to learn that engineering can and should play a key role in creating a more equitable society.

As educational institutions prepare graduates to address social equity in their work, PWOs need to educate their workforces and support this focus through their own training programs, policies, and operations.

Data

There is an exhaustive amount of data at our fingertips that measure environmental factors, community complaints, infrastructure condition, socioeconomic information, and the walkability and bikeability of neighborhoods. Several examples of readily available data include the US Environmental Protection Agency (EPA) air quality data collected at outdoor monitors across the United States, infrastructure condition data collected and reported by the American Society of Civil Engineers, and the walkability index that ranks communities according to their relative walkability as assembled by the EPA. There is also a growing amount of data collected by municipalities to measure these factors at the town, city, and county level. Much of this data can be disaggregated based on census tract or demographic breakdowns. The access to this data provides all agencies with an ability to measure disparities across different neighborhoods. Government agencies need to ensure that they collect the correct data and use it to measure whether their efforts are making a positive difference in the community. Openly sharing this data with others enables private business and other partners to understand community needs and better serve residents.

While government strategies, investments, and activities need to be evidence based and rooted in the analysis of data, decision makers must also understand the stories behind the data. Program managers need to evaluate the causal relationship between actions and results based on the data. Decision makers need to also understand what is happening in the community, the personal stories behind the data, and what factors contribute to positive and negative outcomes. This understanding is developed through taking the time to listen to a diversity of voices and understand their challenges.

For PWOs, most data are geo-coded and reside in the jurisdiction's Geographical Information System. Everything from potholes to road conditions, flooding complaints, streetlight outages, blighted properties, and infrastructure condition can be found on a GIS layer. It is easy to overlay these layers with census-based data and conduct an equity analysis. Then specific areas can be targeted for improvements.

Infrastructure Equity Planning and Design Tools

There are several great tools to help PWOs build more sustainable, resilient, and equitable infrastructure. Envision, Leadership in Energy and Environmental Design (LEED), and WELL Health-Safety Rating (WELL) are building standards and rating systems that measure how projects perform in addressing broad human and societal goals. They score projects based on a triple bottom line analysis of how the projects address environmental, economic, and social equity performance targets.

Envision, developed by the Institute for Sustainable Infrastructure, was born out of a partnership between the American Society for Civil Engineers, American Public Works Association, and American Consulting Engineers Council due to a shared desire to build more sustainable infrastructure that better and more holistically serves our communities. Envision creates a framework for designers to consider a broad array of issues during the planning, design, and construction stages of a project. Issues such as quality of life and the impact of the project on the social fabric of the community are considered. Also considered is how the project team collaborates with the community and stakeholders to build trust and shared ownership of a project's outcomes.

LEED, developed by the US Green Building Council, is focused on the vertical construction and operation of buildings and how they perform in the areas of energy, environment, health, and occupant needs. WELL is a health and safety rating tool used by facility developers to create healthy environments for occupants. According to the EPA, Americans spend approximately 90% of their time indoors (Environmental Protection Agency, 2018). Indoor environmental conditions are important to ensure public health. Building standards need to ensure equity in how buildings are designed for different uses and different communities. LEED and WELL are important rating tools to help building owners, facility planners, and public health officials accomplish this goal. COVID and other public health concerns have created a stronger awareness of this need. Both rating systems encourage the use of natural light, fresh air, nutritional food options, physical activity, bike racks, building materials that do not off-gas VOCs, and other building occupant well-being techniques.

Using these frameworks stretches engineers and planners to think more holistically about the outcomes of a project. The tools require a multidisciplinary approach to planning and designing. Public health professionals, biologists, environmental scientists, community leaders, and others are brought to the table. This broader perspective improves the likelihood of a better and more equitable product. It is important that the advantages brought by these tools are equitably shared for developments and building projects across the full community.

Conclusion

PWOs are the quiet heroes within the community. They pick up the trash, deliver safe drinking water, treat wastewater, build the roads, make sure the streetlights are working, and protect the community from natural disasters. The services provided by PWOs are at the foundation of any thriving community. Historically, the benefits of these services have not been shared equitably across the full community. This has led to creating disadvantages for residents of some neighborhoods. These neighborhoods are disproportionately populated by people of color. Work needs to be done to mitigate the impacts of previous inequitable actions. PWOs need to understand the communities they serve, the variety of needs, and ensure future actions account for equity. Taking the time to understand that different parts of the community have different needs and a full understanding of the benefits and impacts of projects by the different communities needs to be understood and accounted for in project planning. Too often, in trying to solve one problem such as reducing upstream drainage issues in one neighborhood can create downstream flooding in another neighborhood. Utilizing the tools provided in this chapter and taking the time to hear from all voices in the community are the critical first steps in building more sustainable and equitable communities.

Review/Discussion Questions

1. Visit five different neighborhoods in your community (a wealthy residential community, middle class neighborhood, a poor residential community, an old commercial district, and a new commercial district). Describe the different levels of amenities, condition of the infrastructure, and services provided. Are there differences? What are those differences? Do people in these areas share

the same opportunity for success? What recommendations would you make to ensure equity in these different areas?

2. Look at a map of your community and locate the landfill, industrially zoned property, energy plant, and maintenance yards. Are there any remnants of "east siders" in your community?

3. Does your community have a social equity plan? Does your community have a strong public engagement approach and are efforts made by your local government to ensure all voices are heard? What recommendations would you make to strengthen these efforts in your community?

References

American Society for Engineering Education. (2021). *ASEE About.* Retrieved from ASEE: www.asee.org/about-us/the-organization/our-mission

Archer, D. N. (2020). "White Men's Roads Through Black Men's Homes": Advancing Racial Equity Through Highway Reconstruction. *Vanderbilt Law Review, vol. 73,* 1259–1330.

Dr. Dianne Grayce Hendrics, C. G. (2019). *2019 C.NECD – The Collaborative Network for Engineering and Computing Diversity.* Crystal City, VA: American Society for Engineering Education.

Environmental Protection Agency. (2018, July 16). *Report of the Environment.* Retrieved from EPA.Gov www.epa.gov/report-environment/indoor-air-quality

Epanty, E. (2018, October 30). *Virginia Tech Institute for Policy and Governance/Directors Corner.* Retrieved from Virginia Tech Institute for Policy and Governance https://ipg.vt.edu/DirectorsCorner/re--reflections-and-explorations/Reflections103018.html

Fairfax County. (2017). *One Fairfax Policy.* Fairfax, VA: Fairfax County.

Fairfax County. (2020, January). Countywide Strategic Plan. Retrieved from Fairfax County.gov www.fairfaxcounty.gov/strategicplan/

Hugh M. Clark, P. (2017). *Who Rides Public Transportation.* Washington, DC: American Public Transportation Association.

Institute for Sustainable Infrastructure. (2018, April 23). *Madison Metropolitan Sewerage District Pumping Station 15.* Retrieved from Institute for Sustainable Infrastructure https://sustainableinfrastructure.org/project-awards/madison-metropolitan-sewerage-district-pumping-station-15/

Jackson, D. R. (2012). *Designing Healthy Communities.* San Francisco, CA: John Wiley & Sons, Inc.

Julie Nelson, G. H. (2020). Equity Tool Kit. Retrieved from Chicago Public Schools https://equity.cps.edu/tools/changing-the-lights

King County. (2016). *Equity and Social Justice Strategic Plan 2016-2022.* King County, WA: King County.

Stephan Heblich, U. O. (2021). East-Side Story: Historical Pollution and Persistent Neighborhood Sorting. *Journal of Political Economy, vol. 129, no. 5,* 1508–1552.

Steven H. Woolf, D. A. (2017). *Getting Ahead: The Uneven Opportunity Landscape in Northern Virginia.* Richmond, VA: Center on Society and Health and Northern Virginia Health Foundation.

10

PUBLIC PROCUREMENT AND CONTRACT MANAGEMENT FOR ENVIRONMENTAL JUSTICE AND RESILIENCY

Joshua M. Steinfeld

Introduction

The successful SpaceX launches of 2021 featuring a futuristic partnership between Tesla and the Department of Defense presented several implications for thought in the study and practice of the environment and resilience. The ability to reuse previously consumed components of a launch and the commercialization of space exploration demonstrate advancement to an extent that the surplus capability is flowing into the private consumer sector. The resulting technologies and services promise to make the world, or universe, a more habitable place whether it be through new discoveries to take shape in the distant universe, as a haven for survival, or a way to extend the outreach and fulfill the demands of an ever-changing and growing world.

Society faces wicked problems (see Termeer et al., 2019) and the balancing acts required to level set a clean surface are exacerbated by broader forces that pose a challenge to the environment and resiliency, and that is a notion that economies grow exponentially and populations are growing geometrically. The problem that results can be pollution, overcrowding, inequity, and generally a lack of consideration for the environment considering the public and private sectors' need to show results in the near-term; a quarterly, annual, or bi-annual report, or five or ten-year strategic plan. In fact, Olsen's (1965) view on public choice theory espouses an application of the limits of capitalism to an output function by which marginal profit can only be pursued in the presence of overproduction and negative externalities to the physical environment. And Waldo (1982) accurately predicted that the welcoming of the new millennium would demonstrate a characterization of overabundance followed by scarcity.

In a discourse on environmental justice and resiliency the environment includes many facets beyond the physical environment such as achieving equity

DOI: 10.4324/9781003186076-11

and equality in communities comprising the lived environment, and the economic environment. The resiliency framework has also expanded and repositioned to include a major emphasis on supply chain resiliency not solely coastal resiliency, cyber resiliency, or economic resiliency. Meanwhile, the incongruency between the high forces of capitalism and environmentalism is a threat to the achievement of environmental justice and resiliency. Interestingly, similar to a well-functioning business in capitalism, resiliency also involves an iterative state requiring continual collection of data and processing for inputs, data mining and analysis for outputs, tactical planning for reporting and utilizing results, a value engineering, and an evaluation and validation function all providing for agility and cross-cutting capacities.

Perhaps there is no better illustrator than the SpaceX example as it involves numerous uncertainties related to the environment and resiliency. Some concerns arise about the capacity of SpaceX to assume the capabilities of the Department of Navy Space and Warfare Command (SPAWAR) that was scaled into Naval Information Forces Command (NAVIFOR), reflecting a shift to cyber resiliency in the face of government-sponsored air supremacy that has led to additional opportunities in the private sector including the consumer market and contribution of human resiliency with access to space; the potential to launch tens of thousands of satellites is also a benefit. For a moment, when the SpaceX rocket landed safely in reusable condition, the crossfire between economic and environmental drivers resulted in an ultimate moment of national, and if not global resiliency, in the face of a global pandemic that has left many to question what the future looks like.

Government Facets to Resiliency and Partnership: Scope and Opportunities

In Federal Government

The tools and techniques exist in procurement and contracting to mimic the successful launches of SpaceX in a way that contributes to environmental justice and resiliency in all settings and practices for all people. While the Defense Production Act was an acquisition tool utilized by the government to spur businesses to engage in the production process, the SpaceX program features a public-private partnership (PPP). Martin (2018) informs that procurement is a form of partnership as it moves from contracting-out or outsourcing at one extreme and full-fledged PPP at the other; there are now public-public-private partnerships (P4) where multiple levels of government join in.

The landscape is moving toward enhanced resiliency with benefits and shortcomings to environmental justice. The federal acquisition regulations (FAR) is a stringent set of guidelines with particular rules for federal government agencies that govern certain procurement and contracting activities, and discussion is ongoing about alternative purchasing mechanisms and even the potential of undertaking a major revision to the FAR. While the conceptual models reduce cost and improve quality much of the time, there are some areas to be addressed and hence tools such as other transaction authorities (OTAs) are becoming viable mechanisms for scenarios requiring expedited procurement or for which a specific set of FAR guidelines inaptly applies. The trade-offs in favor of resiliency in procuring faster or more agile may be at the haste of the environment in some instances such as a need for research, controls, or improved utilization of goods and services.

The various FAR restrictions that can be known as bureaucratic red tape may actually protect stakeholders to contract who are without a voice such as the physical environment and those relying on the environment for sustenance and business prosperity. FAR guidelines also aim to enhance competition, efficiency, and effectiveness, all potentially leading to more economic resiliency for direct and indirect stakeholders. Economic resiliency can also be tied to physical environment resiliency because it requires substantial resources to address the magnitude of resiliency challenges that exist, considering coastal resiliency issues of sea level rise and supply chain resiliency issues of adaptive manufacturing and dynamic supply systems.

The technology and interlocking effects make it difficult for decision-making at the fringe and so government must make decisions at the face and in the forum. A top level, 50,000-foot view of the public administration is commanded at the face for a foundational approach that sets strategic, tactical, and operational mission guidance and readiness. In the forum, decisions are made in the iterative state of resiliency with data-driven decision-making of data analytics. Government has the resources and human power to optimize for pursuits of resiliency with input and output factors related to environmental justice such as pollution or economic variables. Yet, at the fringe, when government is presented with a problem, aside from the normalness of dealing with the sustainability gearing of the present day, month, or year, it becomes extremely difficult to optimize the environmental and resiliency functions.

Consider the decision of whether to mobilize a destroyer unit instead of an aircraft carrier strike group. There are so many factors to consider from the power sources of the vessels to the number of ships and personnel deployed, aspects of any tertiary missions and logistical impacts which themselves each have an implication for resilience and the environment, and of course combat readiness and economic prowess as it relates to resiliency of democracies. Deeper, the decision to utilize a small, disadvantaged business (SDB) to apply the no-skid on the flight deck of an aircraft carrier may not be the best with risk management and safety as top-line decision criteria. However, without proper incorporation of SDBs into the procurement system and innovative contracting methods then resiliency of the defense industrial base may be challenged. And since small businesses are often-times local businesses or regional businesses, then equity in contracting promotes the progress of the lived environment that is enjoyed by all.

In State and Local Government

For congruency to take place through more involved partnering efforts, state and local governments need to join, especially to harness the advancements regularly gained in the federal government. State governments do operate at the fringe, tiptoeing lines between federal and local jurisdiction, somewhat serving the roles and responsibilities of master organizer. The greatest highlight may be the state's work in transportation, responsible for the infrastructure provision that enables all activity to take shape, and oftentimes through state-wide PPP offices, coordinating partnering activities between federal financing authorities, transportation commissions, state and local agencies, and private businesses including construction (and design) and financing arms.

The infrastructure decisions are never easy, constantly weighing the cost of increasingly traversing the natural environment as construction effects the ecological landscape, leads to demographic and economic shifts locally, and may lead to the enhanced or deteriorated stewardship of the surrounding environment. The effect on resiliency is yet more dynamic in its estimations, oftentimes favoring the build-and-steward model as opposed to the minimalist approach. An example is whether the cultivation of sea aquariums yields gains to sustainability and resiliency of the sea life population through study and stewardship or if it leads to scarcity of wild populations and sustainability at a greater degree.

It could be that the states have the greatest political effect as state boundaries continue to divide public policies on some of the most visible and contentious issues; Tiebout (1956) suggests that residents can vote with their feet. Yet, local government trumps state and federal government on some of the most impactful issues taking place in one's backyard. And federal government supersedes state government when it comes to executive authority. With the brokering powers of states and the potential for regionality, states can be liaisons.

The local government has the power to be project manager at the street-level with its urban planning division. It typically has the most knowledge of the needs and desires of its residents including the preparedness for emergency response and other critical elements of resiliency previously discussed in this book. Since the citizens must live in the confines of their community, the community population is also the best judge of environmental justice. Local government deficiencies surface when disadvantaged groups, disenfranchised voices, or smaller, quiet voices are not heard and allow for the potential dangers to be imposed upon the city, even if the hazards are unknown or inconclusive and remain under continued research. In this sense, the voice of economic reason plays out to the detriment of the public, oftentimes in serving businesses that could yet be better served by state or federal government initiatives that may result in less disruption to daily life; think research and development activities that lead to resiliency capabilities as opposed to beefing up readiness for resiliency by overstocking and merchandising.

Indeed, it is absolutely the local governments that must lead the way in setting the stage for partnering efforts to kick-off meetings. Just as state and local governments hold high the honor and respect of federal government personnel to do a job that provides the pillow-and-blanket for resiliency, the federal government personnel respect the technical expertise and capacities of the local government forces that provide for the range of municipal services and robust local causeways for operations that can be fueled and oiled by local, state, and regional professional associations and bodies that aim to serve and fill gaps between the overlaps.

The Business Sector Corresponding Perspective

Social procurement (Barraket et al., 2016), sustainable procurement (Prier et al., 2016), green procurement (Blome et al., 2014), and socioeconomic contracting (Curry, 2017) have been the agenda setting objectives in public procurement with great potential for businesses to innovate and add value toward these ends. However, these objectives typically exist independently, where priorities and performance targets are sought after without regard to coordinating with other objectives or activities of various stakeholders. For example, businesses may invest substantial amounts of money innovating products and services without knowing if the government will assign weighting and value to these additional features in the solicitation and proposal evaluation. If government is not willing to pay more for innovative products and services, or does not mobilize its logistical resources for coordinating activities that enable innovative products and services to benefit government, then companies may lack the incentive to innovate. It is innovation that provides for products and services that support goals in environmental justice and resiliency.

There are also contracting mechanisms that are attempts to improving equity in the vendor and supplier marketplace. More and more, a tie is being made between equity in source selection and equitable outcomes for stakeholder communities that serve or are served by businesses. Conversely, the distribution of public goods and services, which inevitably impacts the source and vendor selection because different businesses specialize in particular areas, can also be evaluated according to equity. The government sometimes has set structures in place to promote contracting with women-owned, minority-owned, and veteran-owned businesses, both the business sector and government sector should not express frustrations regarding any additional steps that need to be taken in forming partnerships with women, minorities, and veterans to qualify to submit bids and proposals for government work.

These structures are in place to address problems that exist, specifically a lack of equity and diversity in the supplier marketplace, leading to procurement issues that result in disadvantaged communities, a scarcity of products and services to bring to market, and a lack of competition and subcontracting efforts along the supply chain. However, businesses are often confused about the signal being sent by government through its procurement and contracting activities. And, when small businesses gear up to compete for and deliver in performing to government contracts, there is a possibility that the comprehensive efforts may not lead to a profitable project, or worse could leave a company in financial turmoil due to losses on a given project. Businesses and governments need to work together to determine the type of work or contracts that various businesses are best suited for while addressing areas that can be improved.

More so, supplier diversity has become vital for society in establishing a sustainable and resilient supply chain. Steinfeld (2022–forthcoming) exemplifies the importance of supply chain resiliency against a backdrop of uncertainty amid COVID-19 and an intensified global discourse among world power nations. Just as governments are modifying their approach to public procurement and contracting in fulfilling need during supply shortages and for critical supplies such as personal protective equipment (PPE), businesses may not be on the same page as business administrations were organized according to government structures of the past. While government procurement practitioners may be willing and ready for more advanced, constructive discussions with vendors and contractors such as at informal gatherings during pre-solicitation, businesses may not know where to seek these interactions.

A host of professional associations, organizations, and bodies, some operating by government entities, exist to serve businesses such as the small business development liaisons of the Department of Defense that aim to guide small businesses through the process of bidding and winning federal government contract awards. Other associations may focus on initiatives of regional economic development or local entrepreneurship, and while these associations oftentimes offer training programs or provide resources that connect dots, there is still a need for thorough advocacy that takes businesses through the entire contracting lifecycle. Furthermore, businesses may win a contract award to perform government work but may lack the ability or be under-resourced in pursuing subsequent work opportunities, especially while simultaneously performing to a government contract.

The obstacles faced by SDB, minority-owned, women-owned, and veteran-owned businesses may be twofold. On one hand, these businesses face the same challenges that all businesses face, such as identifying and fulfilling opportunities for contractual work. On the other hand, disadvantaged businesses face an exacerbated set of problems due to disadvantages with regards to socioeconomic status (SES). This may inhibit not only social interactions between buyers and sellers of goods and services but also make it difficult to execute the administrative functions required for government work including drafting proposals, quality assurance, and accounting systems.

Large corporations can assume leading roles and responsibilities to include SDB into the supply chain through subcontracting or redesign of product or service production and delivery. The result may be cost savings and other efficiencies, including innovations, for the corporation who can focus its efforts on assembly, or productive areas of competitive advantage, and let other smaller companies focus on what they may do best. The more supply chain participants, the more likely it is to achieve resiliency in the form of adaptive capacity that requires ingenuity and fungibility by use of component and subcomponent systems design.

Steinfeld (2017) builds on the notion that governments and businesses can work together via a heightened sense of mutual reliance, camaraderie, and partnership. In fact, resiliency relies on it, especially in uncertain times and crises. For example, during the COVID-19 pandemic, the corresponding reliance between sectors was paramount; the government could not provide services while businesses and the labor force were not working. And businesses found it nearly impossible to operate without the supportive structures of government.

Conclusion

To make strides toward a more collaborative approach that facilitates information exchange and equal participation, some sacrifices need to be made in the short term such as the willingness of a business to take extra steps to abide by government directives intended to address issues of environmental justice and resiliency, or the willingness of larger corporations to share in the success with smaller, disadvantaged companies. From the government standpoint, an emphasis on product and service delivery, and more trust in its procurement and contracting professionals, may lead to efficiencies and effectiveness that promotes resiliency measures. Both businesses and governments should embrace a more open forum for product and service delivery, moving away from cutthroat competition that limits collaborative engagement and being willing to accept modest levels of vulnerability to take the guard down and get to business. It is thus espoused a model for environmental justice and resiliency given uncertainty relies upon a partnered, advocacy approach that is diverse, equitable, and inclusive.

Collaborative approaches insinuate a willingness to be vulnerable at times and even take small risks when trailblazing new pathways to get the same old goods and services in this age of uncertainty and prevailing foci on resiliency. For innovation to take place, government and business need to be willing to assume postmodern approaches at times (see Miller, 2002). This means valuing the holistic and seeking creative ways to provide and fulfill opportunities for partnering between sectors, despite conventional wisdom that suggested the public and private sector are necessarily counterparties.

The postmodernist views both sides of the coin and follows the lineage of decision actions for an understanding of how one decision can have cascading, overlapping, or layering effects that require the utmost integration and coordination of human capital, technological resources, and operational activity. Essentially, each stakeholder to a contract has an opportunity to be an agent of change, or a contributor, by critically examining government and business activities and seeking to leverage partnering that may provide for agility, versatility, and flexibility to engage procurement and contracting in ways that promote environmental justice and resiliency.

Discussion Questions

1. What specific public procurement and contracting decision actions can be taken to promote diversity, equity, and inclusion?
2. What are performance measures or indicators that diversity, equity, and inclusion are being improved and leading to successful outcomes for SDB businesses?
3. Who are the stakeholders that contribute to or are affected by aspects of environmental justice and resiliency? How can these stakeholders play a role in procurement and contracting?
4. Can you identify and discuss PPP that have had the effect of improving both public service delivery and equity across communities?
5. What are steps that government and business may take together to pursue partnerships that better equip society for risk and uncertainty?

References

Barraket, Josephine, Keast, Robyn, & Craig Furneaux. (2016). *Social Procurement and New Public Governance*. New York, NY: Routledge.

Blome, Constantin, Hollos, Daniel, & Antony Paulraj. (2014). Green Procurement and Green Supplier Development: Antecedents and Effects on Supplier Performance. *International Journal of Production Research* 52(1): 32–49.

Curry, William Sims. (2017). *Government Contracting: Promises and Perils* (2nd Ed.). New York, NY: Routledge.

Martin, Lawrence. (2016). Making Sense of Public-Private Partnerships (P3s). *Journal of Public Procurement* 16(2): 191–207.

Miller, Hugh. (2002). *Postmodern Public Policy*. Albany, NY: State University of New York Press.

Olsen, Mancur. (1965). *The Logic of Collective Action: Public Goods and the Theory of Groups*. Cambridge: Harvard University Press.

Prier, Eric, Schwerin, Ed, & Cliff McCue. (2016). Implementation of Sustainable Procurement Practices and Policies: A Sorting Framework. *Journal of Public Procurement* 16(3): 312–346.

Steinfeld, Joshua. (2017). The What, Who, and How of Public Procurement: Job Functions Performed and Managed by Professionals. In K.V. Thai (Ed.), *Global Public Procurement Theories and Practices* (pp. 311–335), New York, NY: Springer.

Steinfeld, Joshua. (2022–forthcoming). Fulfill Need Leveraging Public Procurement and Contract Management. In A.Y. Ni and M. Van Wart (Eds.), *Building Business-Government Relations: A Skills Approach* (2nd Ed.). New York, NY: Routledge.

Termeer, Catrien, Dewilf, Art, and Robbert Biesbroek. (2019). A Critical Assessment of the Wicked Problem Concept: Relevance and Usefulness for Policy Science and Practice. *Policy and Society* 38(2): 167–179.

Tiebout, Charles. (1956). A Pure Theory of Local Expenditures. *Journal of Political Economy* 64(5): 416–424.

Waldo, Dwight. (1982). *The Enterprise of Public Administration*. Novato, CA: Chandler and Sharp Publishers.

CONCLUSION

Building a Justice-Focused Resilient Path Forward

Celeste Murphy-Greene

This book documents the environmental justice challenges our society faces in these uncertain times. The evidence is clear, the impacts of climate change are real and the burdens disproportionately fall on those least able to cope with the social, economic, and environmental stresses caused by extreme weather. Additionally, the COVID-19-induced pandemic has shined the light on the many "pre-existing" social, economic, environmental, and public health issues that have been present for decades. Both COVID-19 and climate change exacerbate the issues many communities struggle to cope with already, such as the impacts of urban heat islands (UHIs) and a lack of trust with the medical community. To truly achieve environmental justice, an equity and justice-focused resilience strategy is imperative for all communities.

The environmental and social challenges we face as a country and global community in the 21st century are real, but as this book has demonstrated, the solutions are within our reach. The progress achieved since the environmental justice movement began in the 1980s is evidence that hard to reach goals are attainable. The integration of environmental justice into federal, state, and local government policies and priorities demonstrates the true commitment to this important issue by all levels of government. In the past 40 years, the environmental justice movement has expanded from its grassroots beginnings to become a national priority, as demonstrated by the current US Environmental Protection Agency, The White House's Justice40 Plan, and the commitment all federal agencies and departments have made by integrating environmental justice into their mission and actions plans. States are taking a lead in addressing environmental justice at the state level through state policies and initiatives. However, local communities will continue to play a large role in implementing justice-focused resilience strategies to address the growing threat of climate change and to reign in COVID-19.

DOI: 10.4324/9781003186076-12

This book demonstrates the linkages between the issues of public health, climate change, clean energy, emergency management, public works, smart cities, procurement and contract management, and a justice-focused approach to resiliency. Resilient communities are built by an inclusive and equity-focused approach to each of the previously mentioned issues. For communities to be truly resilient and have the capacity to withstand the environmental challenges on the horizon, they must focus on the needs of the vulnerable members, who may lack the capacity and resources to cope with the challenges that many with resources are able to handle. Communities must also utilize existing resources such as community organizations and institutions, such as churches, schools, civic leagues, and even barber shops to build trust with government and medical professionals. The ability of these community resources to communicate with residents about the benefits of the COVID-19 vaccine to help overcome vaccine hesitancy or help engage community members about the impacts of climate change such as sea-level rise, cannot be underestimated. As this book has highlighted, these trusted community resources are excellent in educating community members and sharing information.

As this book reveals, past policies and practices such as redlining and the Tuskegee Public Health Study, have lasting impacts on society that are still present today. These past discriminatory practices and policies continue to impact minorities' trust in government and the medical establishment. Working to rebuild trust in government institutions, such as the Public Health Service and city planning departments will take concerted effort and work by policy makers at all levels of government. In essence, we cannot move forward to fully address resiliency, without truly recognizing the impact of past discriminatory practices on minority populations. A justice-focused approach to resiliency includes recognition of historic inequities, such as redlining, and addresses the impacts such policies and practices currently have on community members, such as the dangers of Urban Heat Islands (UHIs) and the disproportionate impact UHIs have on minority low-income residents.

Justice-focused resilient strategies involve an inclusive community-based approach. This approach is currently in practice with Richmond, Virginia's RVAgreen2050 plan, which involves community-based organizations, such as GrounworkRVA, working to address the impacts of climate change by involving at-risk youth in green infrastructure plans such as tree planting and landscaping in urban areas. This approach is also utilized in California's local clean energy initiatives such as RYSE in Northern California's Bay Area. Additionally, cities such as Norfolk, Virginia, which is currently dealing with impacts of sea-level rise, have included an equity and justice lens in the city's emergency management and resilient strategies.

In conclusion, the path to creating resilient communities is one based on transparency, openness, recognizing past discriminatory practices, understanding the inequitable burdens pollution and extreme weather place on vulnerable populations, and seeking involvement from all community members to address these inequities. This participatory approach will help rebuild trust in government and non-government organizations working to address community needs. While environmental justice has made much progress in the past 40 years, there is still much work to be done to help build strong resilient communities for all residents. This book provides strategies to help build more resilient communities using a justice lens. It's now up to us to put these strategies into action.

INDEX

Printed in the United States
by Baker & Taylor Publisher Services